Here's what writing and publishing experts are saying about

The Publishing Game: Bestseller in 30 Days

"*The Publishing Game* provides a day-by-day book promotion outline that will accurately lead you every step of the way. Now you can be assured that you are doing every possible thing to promote your book and you are doing it in the right order. This book IS your marketing plan."—**Dan Poynter, *The Self-Publishing Manual***

"If anyone can make a game out of publishing, Fern Reiss can. I wish more publishers would not only follow her step-by-step lesson plan but read this book BEFORE they start rolling the publishing dice."–**Jan Nathan, Executive Director, Publishers Marketing Association**

"A very useful step-by-step overview of the daunting task of getting published."—**Carl Lennertz, BookSense, American Booksellers Association**

"Positively awesome! Every writer should buy this book." —**Rick Frishman, *Guerrilla Marketing for Writers***

"A step-by-step, day-by-day roadmap from complete unknown to bestseller. Packed with excellent resources. Follow every step and your chances of hitting the bigtime go dramatically skyward. Keep this book in the "use it all the time" section of your bookshelf."—**Shel Horowitz, *Grassroots Marketing: Getting Noticed in a Noisy World***

"Packed with tips, tricks, names and websites, this day-by-day plan will have you on your way to winning the publishing game before you even know it."
—**Mary Westheimer, www.BookZone.com, the Net's largest publishing community**

"A wealth of targeted instruction on how to drive your book to success. I especially like the bullet point presentation method; it makes action steps easy to follow and fast to review. This book is a useful addition to the literature on the subject."—**Marilyn Ross, *Jump Start Your Book Sales***

"A powerful addition to the classics in the field."
—**Pat Bell, *THE Prepublishing Handbook***

Other Books by Fern Reiss

The Publishing Game: Publish a Book in 30 Days

The Publishing Game: Find an Agent in 30 Days

Terrorism and Kids: Comforting Your Child

The Infertility Diet: Get Pregnant and
Prevent Miscarriage

Other Offerings from
Peanut Butter and Jelly Press

Literary Agents Kit

Sell Your Books to Corporations

Top Amazon Reviewers

Independent Bookstores Publicity Kit

Email Newsletter Kit

Syndicate Yourself Kit

Special Reports Kit

The Publishing Game:
Bestseller in 30 Days

by **Fern Reiss**

Peanut Butter and Jelly Press
Boston, Massachusetts

Copyright © 2003 by Fern Reiss. Printed in the United States of America.

To receive a **free weekly email newsletter** on books and independent publishing, send email to:

> newsletter@PublishersAdvocate.com

For more **information and resources for writers and publishers**, visit our website at www.PublishingGame.com.

Attention corporations, writing organizations and writing conferences: If you'd like to find out about using books, booklets, or book excerpts as fundraisers or premiums, please contact the publisher:

Peanut Butter and Jelly Press, LLC
P.O. Box 590239
Newton, Massachusetts 02459-0002
(617)630-0945
info@PublishingGame.com
www.PBJPress.com
SAN 299-7444

Library of Congress Cataloging-in-Publication Data

Reiss, Fern.
  The publishing game: bestseller in 30 days / by Fern Reiss.
      p. cm.
  Includes bibliographical references and index.
  ISBN 1-893290-88-3
1. Publishing. 2. Marketing. I. Title.
Pending
                              CIP
              10 9 8 7 6 5 4 3 2 1

Dedication

Words can not express my eternal love and thanks to my incredible husband, Jonathan, who has been the best Mom (not to mention husband and webmaster) while I've been barricaded in my office writing; and to my three wonderful home schooled children, Benjamin, Daniel, and Ariel, who, though they still have not quite grasped the concept of "Don't bother Mommy, she's working," continue to interrupt me for the most fascinating of reasons.

Thank you to my parents, for putting up with me while writing my way through what was supposed to be our vacation visit to Florida Thanks to the wonderful staff at Seattle's Best Coffee, to whom I feel I should be paying rent for permanent occupancy of the corner booth.

Thank you to everyone who made this book possible, especially my cover designer, Mayapriya Long (When do I get the cookies?) Thanks to the many folks on pub-forum whose irreverent expertise on every subject continues to astound me. A special thanks to all those who helped in getting *Publishers Advocate* launched, particularly Peter Goodman.

Finally, thank you to the many supportive readers of my books. If you buy a copy now, this book, too, will be a bestseller. (If not, could you maybe ask your library and favorite corporation to buy a handful?)

Love to all,

Fern

Contents

Introduction

⊂⊱ ⊰⊃

Everyone wants to create a bestseller.

You can do it. In 30 days.

Whether you've just sold your book and are wondering if it will make you rich—or you've published it yourself and are wondering how to get those copies out of your garage and into the hands of book buyers—this is the book for you. *You* are the only person who can make your book a bestseller. And you *can* do it yourself—in the next 30 days.

This book won't teach you to *write* a bestseller. It will teach you to take your book—the one you've already written—and make it fly off the shelves. If you've published it yourself, it will also teach you how to get your book *onto* those shelves in the first place.

If your book was just accepted by a large publishing house, this book is for you. Publishers—even the big fancy New York publishers, the ones who still occasionally treat clients to lunch—won't do your publicity. They won't send you on a book tour or sell thousands of copies to big corporations. They no longer have the time to mentor you through the bookselling process. They probably won't even call Oprah for you. So if you want your book to have a longer shelf-life than cottage cheese, you'll need to promote your book yourself. This book will teach you how.

If you're an independent publisher—that is, if you've decided to publish yourself, and have gotten as far as the books-in-your-garage stage—this book is critical. Nobody can get those books out of the garage but you! If you follow the step-by-step directions in this book, you can make a bundle of money. Big publishers can't touch the "small" books that will only sell 5,000 copies, because it's not worth it for them. But you can—and you can make a tidy profit on it. There are over 50,000 small publishers in the United States today, generating an estimated annual $14 billion in book sales. You can be one of them.

You can move faster. You can sell fewer (and still make money.) You can make enough to give up your day job.

You just need to know how.

That's where this book comes in. I'm going to take you, step by step, through the process of creating a bestselling book. In the next 30 days, you'll learn how to get your book into bookstores, libraries, corporations, book clubs, catalogs, and the hands of the public.

Can my book really be a bestseller?

Bestselling means different things to different people: Some books sell only a few thousand copies and make the bestseller lists, while others sell many more but never make the lists. To further complicate the situation, there are now several different lists purporting to be *the* bestseller list, and all are different.

I can't guarantee that your book will appear on one of these lists—or that you'll sell hundreds of thousands of copies. But if you're an author whose efforts result in wildly successful book sales, you guarantee that your *next* book will command much more money. And if you have independently published and you sell even as few as 5,000 books at $10 profit each, that's $50,000. (If you've got two books, that's $100,000.) Not bad for 30 days work. And anyone—repeat, anyone—who follows these guidelines should be able to sell at least that many. Some of you will sell a whole lot more.

The only exceptions are if you're writing fiction, poetry, or children's literature. Many of these same steps can be followed—but the results are not as certain as they are with nonfiction books. Still, any well-written, carefully edited, nicely designed and professionally covered book, combined with this 30-day plan, will sell many books. If you've written a novel, try using this book too—but bear in mind that your mileage may vary.

If it's so easy, why doesn't everyone do it?

That's a good question: If it's so easy to sell lots of books, why doesn't everyone do it?

Selling books takes time. It takes energy. It takes motivation and passion. Most authors and publishers have all that.

What they don't usually have is a *plan*.

Every long-range goal requires a plan. If you're going to compete in a marathon, you make up a training schedule: Run 2 miles the first week, run 5 miles the 2nd week, etc. If you're going to apply to graduate school, you make up a list of requirements: take the GREs, send for applications, write the essays. If you want to lose weight, you find a diet, and (try to) follow it.

If you want to create a bestseller, you need a day-by-day plan so you know where you're heading, and what you need to do each day to get there.

This book is that plan.

Why should I read this particular book?

There are a great many books available on how to publicize your books (so that people will go into bookstores looking for them) and a handful on how to work with wholesalers and stores to make sure that your books are *in* bookstores (so that when the people go looking for your book, they can find it.) There are very few books that describe both the in and out of this process. But if you don't know how to do both—get the books *into* the bookstores, and then create a demand that keeps the books moving *out* of the bookstores—you can't sell books.

More importantly, if you don't know the sequence in which to do things, then *even if you've read other books describing what to do*, you won't be approaching your targets in the right order. There's nothing worse than doing a fantastic seminar attended by dozens of enthusiastic readers—and then discovering that the bookstore doesn't have books to sell them; getting a plum article in a major national magazine months before your books have made it into the bookstores; or watching the UPS man struggling under the weight of large boxes coming back towards your garage, because the returns are coming in before the publicity packets have gone out. Unfortunately, these disasters can occur *even if* you're using a mainstream publisher. This book will give you a day-by-day, step-by-step plan so that that won't happen.

This book won't teach you everything you might want to know about marketing a book to bestsellerdom: We're not trying to be comprehensive. What it will do is to take you by the hand and lead you, step by step and day by day, through the *first thirty days* of things you should do. There are many other things you can do—but if you've followed the steps faithfully, your book will already be launched on the road to the bestseller status. After that, you're on your own.

Is this standard publishing wisdom?

No. Much of the advice in this book is, shall we say, maverick. I have firm opinions on how this process should be done—and my opinions don't always jibe with the "accepted wisdom" of the rest of the book world. (On the other hand, my books are selling pretty well—and that's not true for many publishers in the industry.)

Unlike many, I firmly believe that *any* well-written nonfiction book can be a bestseller. I also believe in selling books no-returns, something most publishers would like, but don't do because they believe they will make less money (I think you'll make more). And I don't have a whole lot of faith in spending money on advertising, though a lot of people, particularly those on Madison Avenue, disagree with me. Given a choice, I vote for spending your money on publicity—postcards, mailings to bookstores and libraries, fax campaigns to the media, travel so that you can speak at seminars and conferences in far-flung places—rather than on paid advertisements.

So, no, this isn't standard publishing wisdom. But it works.

How do I use this book?

The content in this book is arranged chronologically. You follow the day-to-day assignments and end up with a super seller in 30 days.

I've broken the plan down into five day chunks, so that you can still enjoy your weekends—but if you prefer, you can work straight through, and really be done with the whole plan in a month. (I recommend the six-week plan, though; part of the fun of playing with a book is that your time is your own, but if you're working seven days a week you will be too exhausted to enjoy it.)

Though this plan is designed to be used in 30 days, ideally you should do the first week's work and then take a short break before starting the second week's assignments. You'll be accomplishing tasks the first week that require set-up time— such as setting up a website and printing postcards—and you probably won't have the results for several days. So plan to spend five days on the book, and then take a breather for a week. The remainder of the tasks can be accomplished as a unit.

As much as possible, do the activities on the day that they're assigned. Sometimes you might have to jiggle the tasks: If your postcards take a week longer to be printed than mine did, or you hear back from independent booksellers sooner than I assumed, rearrange your schedule accordingly.

Keep in mind, too, that your strengths may not be mine: It may take you longer to do certain steps, and less time to do others. Budget your time accordingly.

Many of the day's assignments, particularly after the first week, won't require a full day to complete, and can be sandwiched in between the other responsibilities in your life. You can follow this book and keep your day job (though if you're diligent, maybe soon you won't have to!)

Some people will find 30 days just the right amount of time for this plan. Others will find that it takes them somewhat longer. It doesn't really matter how many days it takes you: What's important are the results.

So get going. And don't forget to write and tell me whether you've been able to follow this book to make *your* book into a 30 day success story.

What if I'm the author but not the publisher?

As the author, you can follow almost all of the steps in this book, regardless of whether or not you've published your book yourself. Even the biggest publishers don't help much with publicity these days, and many of their books don't stay on the shelves longer than about eight months. If you hope your book will make a lot of money and stay in bookstores, you'll need to spend your own time and resources doing promotion.

Whether or not you've published yourself, you can contact the media, work with bookstores and libraries, organize your own speaking tour, and initiate large sales to organizations and corporations. You can syndicate yourself, sell to catalogs and the home shopping network, and talk to the media. You can get involved online, join associations, enter your book in contests, and sell special reports.

As a published author you may need to coordinate some of these activities with your publisher—but your publisher won't care if you go off and drum up your own book sales. (Though they will be surprised. Most authors sit back and wait for their publishers to do this work—and eight months later, they're disappointed to discover that they've earned very little money and their books are on the remainder tables at the dollar store.)

As an author, the most important thing to do is to get a good discount on your books from the publisher. A smart publisher will sell you as many of your books as you want at wholesale prices—because you're going to do your utmost to sell them. If it's not too late, make sure you write this into your contract.

So get out there and hit the pavement. And next time, consider publishing independently. You'll spend more time, but you'll make a whole lot more money.

What if my book is already published?

A great many people ask me what they can do if their book has already been published. I haven't seen many wonderful books on how to handle an old or backlist title. But although you won't be able to follow this 30-day plan exactly—some of the items you'll already have completed, others it will be too late to attempt—if you've written a book that's already published, you can still follow many of the steps in this book. (In fact, unless you call attention to it, many people won't notice how long ago you published the book.) Keeping your book active will keep it selling. And a good "backlist" title can sell forever—at the rate of several thousand copies per year.

If this sounds impossible to you, take a look at my first book, *The Infertility Diet: Get Pregnant and Prevent Miscarriage*. It was first published in 1999—and still sells at a steady rate of several thousand copies per year, bringing in at least $30,000 in net income each year. Not only that, but I continue to get new reviews for it, some of these in very prestigious publications. As long as I have the energy to market it, I expect it to continue to sell for at least the next five years.

So get to work. You, too, can be a bestselling—and well paid—author and publisher.

What should I do beforehand?

The 30-day plan assumes that you already have a quality book underway, and you're reading this as advance preparation—or you already have a finished book, at your publisher or in your garage. Either way, this book will prove useful.

If you haven't gotten as far as the books in the garage, start with a publishing primer. *The Publishing Game: Bestseller in 30 Days* will "catch you up" on a number of issues, but if you have no idea how to submit an RFQ to printers or how to find a cover artist, you need to start there and save this book for a little later. Try the prequel to this book, *The Publishing Game: Publish a Book in 30 Days* for a day-by-day plan on independently publishing your book. But go ahead and read this book now anyway—it always helps to know what's coming up next.

One thing you should be certain to do, before you finalize your book title, is to obtain the domain name for the book, to make it easy for people to find and order your book online.

Keep in mind, too, that Ingram, the largest book wholesaler, allows only 30 characters in its title field: Try to limit your title to 30 characters or fewer. And most directories list books by title, rather than by author—so try to start your title with your most important keyword.

Tell your cover artist to plan on doing a postcard-sized file of your cover as soon as you've selected a postcard printer, so that you can have postcards printed easily.

If you haven't yet printed your books, try to win an award now, so that you can include an award sticker on the cover of the book—a tactic sure to increase sales, even if the reader hasn't heard of the award. A detailed list of awards and their deadlines appears on Day #15.

If you're publishing the book yourself, we also assume that you've already done the legwork to set up your publishing house legally. Before you proceed in marketing your book, make sure your publishing house is set up correctly from a legal standpoint. That means registering your company, acquiring the appropriate permits and paperwork and applying for a bank account in the name of your publishing house. Make sure you can accept credit cards—credit card customers spend an estimated 15-30% more than cash customers, and are much more likely to buy.

Be particularly careful in choosing your publishing house name—check directories (including *Literary Marketplace*) to make sure that the name isn't already in use, and make sure you can buy the publishing house name as a domain name for your website.

You also need to organize a workspace, contract for (both regular and toll-free) telephone, and get a computer and a fax machine. There are many books on starting businesses; consult one of these for detailed information on how to do this in your state. And consult *The Publishing Game: Publish a Book in 30 Days* for details on setting up your publishing house and printing your books. You might also check out the website of Ivan Hoffman (www.ivanhoffman.com), a publishing lawyer who features many informative articles on various legal aspects of publishing. Do *not* start marketing your book until your business is set up. Setting up your business can be done in just a few days if you hustle.

How much money should I spend?

That completely depends on you. In this business, you can spend as much—or as little—as you like. (The joke in the industry—How do you make a small fortune in publishing?

Start with a large fortune!—does not need to be true, though it certainly can be if you're not careful.)

In thinking about your budget, there are several things to consider. If you're the author but not the publisher, determine how much of your own money you want to allocate to publicizing your book. (Remember that, if you haven't published the book yourself, you might not recoup this money.) If you're the publisher, remember that you may experience a cash-flow problem since printers (and others) demand advance payment, but wholesalers' standard terms are 90 days or more. If you don't already have a business, you will incur some expenses to set that up, and some additional expenses in equipment and services. You may want to pay to have someone else answer your phones, orchestrate your publicity, or handle your book fulfillment (taking, packing, and shipping orders), or you may prefer to do those tasks in-house, incurring additional work but saving the expense.

Keep in mind that you'll need to pay for big items (printing galleys and books), smaller expenses (joining associations, entering contests, printing postcards, purchasing publicity services or media lists, attending conferences) and operating expenses (rent if you have a separate office, telephone, postage). Some of these items can be skimped on or eliminated, and some you can pay others to do, but you'll need to decide which items are essential for you.

(See Appendix G: Sample Budget for more on this.)

One final word before you begin

Finally, remember to have fun. Whether you're an author who is determined to have your book make a difference or a publisher who is tired of being told you can't, it *is* possible to create a bestseller, make money at it, and enjoy the process. Publishing truly is a game. So have fun!

Week Number One

CR ଔ

This week you'll:

- Make sure you have the basic components your book needs—ISBN, ABI, EAN barcode, CIP data

- Decide on a discount schedule and terms

- Plan your future titles

- Chart your progress

- Send your book for reviews

- Submit your book to the wholesalers

- Generate quotations

- Design and order postcards

- Set up a website for the book

Day Number 1

Today you'll catch up on all the things that you should have done already—but may have forgotten. You'll check on your **ISBN, ABI, EAN barcode,** and **CIP data.** You'll decide on a **discount schedule and terms.** You'll **plan your future titles.** And you'll establish a **progress chart.**

ISBN, ABI, EAN Barcode, and CIP

Here's how to sell your books to bookstores and libraries:

- Make sure you have applied for an ISBN (International Standard Book Number) for your book. You can choose to pay for either 10 ISBNs or 100. I strongly recommend securing 100 ISBNs, even though it is more expensive, because it will give you the professional appearance you need. Detailed information on the ISBN is included in Appendix B: ISBN Numbers and Bar Codes.

- Make sure you have submitted the ABI (Advance Book Information) form to R.R. Bowker. This will ensure that your book is included in *Books in Print* and Bowker's other directories. Detailed information on the ABI is included in Appendix C: ABI Form.

- Make sure that your book has a Bookland EAN bar code on the back cover. Your cover designer should be able to take care of this for you.

Detailed information on the Bookland EAN barcode is included in Appendix B: ISBN Numbers and Bar Codes.

- Make sure that the book has Cataloging-in-Publication (CIP) data from the Library of Congress. Certain libraries will buy your book *sight unseen* based on this CIP data—so don't neglect this step! Quality Books also offers unofficial cataloging but it won't generate these automatic sales. Detailed information on CIP is included in Appendix D: Library Numbers and Cataloging.

- If the book has not yet been printed, make sure that you insert information on *all* your books and upcoming related products on the book's order form, which should be printed as the last page of the book. This way you won't miss out on potential sales of current and future books and products.

Discount Schedule and Terms

You will need to decide on a discount schedule and terms. Here are some things to consider:

- You can offer one set of terms to wholesalers, and another set of terms to retailers, but you are legally required to offer the same terms within a category; thus, if you offer one wholesaler a certain discount, you must offer *all* wholesalers that discount. You have some flexibility in that you can set different terms based on quantities purchased—for example, "55% discount on orders of 40 books or more; 40% discount on orders of fewer than 40 books."

- "Standard" terms of wholesalers are 55% discount (that is, you retain only 45% of the retail price of the book); you pay shipping of orders (to the wholesaler) and shipping of returns (when they send books back); all books are sold on consignment (that is, the books can be returned to you at any time and for any reason); and they will send payment in 90 (which usually means at least 120) days. Standard discounts to exclusive distributors are upwards of 65%.

- You don't have to agree to the standard terms. You can offer less than the 55% discount (some publishers set their discount schedule at 20%); insist that they pay shipping via Fed Ex Ground collect or UPS collect in one or both directions; sell books non-returnable, rather than on consignment; and demand prepayment for all orders. Or, you can agree to standard terms on some issues, and set your own terms on others: It's up to you to decide which issues are most important to you and which terms you can live with.

- In thinking about discount terms, one trick is to set the price of your book high enough that you can easily *afford* 55% discount. (All my titles, for example, are priced between $14.95 and $24.95, and that gives me enough slack to generously offer 55% terms to my largest buyers.)

- Understand that wholesalers will order anything that the bookstores or libraries request, *regardless of your terms*. While it is true that *bookstores* might be reluctant to order a book which is non-returnable, as long as bookstores and libraries order it, wholesalers will stock it. That means that as long as you are generating sufficient demand for your book by readers, you don't have to worry about your terms being unacceptable to the wholesalers.

- Consider the sample budget in Appendix G: Sample Budget to help in figuring out how much your publishing venture will cost, and what sorts of discount terms you can afford.

- Plan what you want your STOP discount to be. STOP stands for Single Title Order Plan. You can list your STOP discount with the ABA Book Buyer's Handbook, so that bookstores will be able to easily order one copy of your book, directly from you, when a customer comes in and requests it. The bookstore will simply send you a check and order; you ship the book and there's no more paperwork involved. Most publishers set their STOP at 20% discount plus shipping. Since this is a service bookstores provide customers on special orders, there's no reason to give a larger discount; STOP orders do not usually lead to larger orders. Fill this out as part of the ABI.

- To find the most current information on what terms independent publishers are setting, join the fledgling trade association, Publishers Advocate (See the Publishers Advocate appendix or www.PublishersAdvocate.com.)

Plan Your Future Titles

Unfortunately, many sectors of the publishing industry—including, but not limited to, Ingram, the Library of Congress, and Bowker—won't take you seriously when you're starting out as a publisher.

To combat what amounts to monopolistic exclusion from many desirable services, you'll need to appear bigger and further along than you currently are. Here's how:

- On your block of 100 ISBNs, write down a list of possible upcoming titles. Plan at least 10-15 titles, and include the names of various. (different) authors: You, your spouse, your mother, etc. You're not actually committing to publishing any of these books.

- Type up a formal letter, on your publishing company letterhead, that says "Forthcoming titles from (name of your press)"

- List each title, author, and ISBN. You can also include page counts, editions (hardcover or softcover), and retail prices.

- Now, with several titles firmly in hand, you're eligible for a wide array of programs that exclude smaller presses. Include your list when you're contacting:

  o Ingram (about being carried by this wholesaler)

  o Library of Congress (when you apply for CIP data)

  o Bowker, and particularly Literary Market Place (LMP) (to be listed in this annual directory; they require publishers to produce at least three new titles annually)

  o The ABA Book Buyers Handbook (which bookstores use to order single titles directly; they require at least 7 titles if you want to be listed)

Make a Progress Chart

Now, put a big piece of graph paper on your wall. Put the upcoming weeks (for at least six months) along the bottom of the graph; put the quantities of books, in 25 book increments, along the left side. Every time you make a book sale, add it to the previous books sold and mark the total on your graph. This works as encouragement to dieters and budgeters—so why not for book sellers? As the numbers of books flying out of the garage increases, you'll be more and more motivated to sell more books—and the process will take on a life of its own.

Day Number 2

Today you'll send your book out for **reviews**. You'll also send your book to **wholesalers.**

Get Reviews

Sending your book out to reviewers is a crucial step. Without reviews from major journals, you are seriously limiting your sales to bookstores and particularly libraries, regardless of the quality of your book. If you can score a review in *BookList* or *Library Journal*, you automatically guarantee several thousand sales to libraries. The good news is that, with a good manuscript, reviews are not that difficult to get. Here are some issues to consider and things to do:

- Send your review copy immediately, because getting a review takes time. Most of the journals work at least three to six months in advance. If you are an independent publisher, make sure you enclose a cover letter that tells the reviewer your publication date (which has nothing to do with the date your books are printed, and which you can arbitrarily set to be whenever you want) and make sure that publication date is sufficiently far ahead—at least three to six months off—that the journals will have time to schedule the review of your book. Try not to schedule your publication date for the fall or spring; those are publishing's busiest seasons, and your books are less likely to be reviewed then.

- Traditionally, publishers send reviewers "advance galleys" or "advance review copies" (ARCs)—the terms are identical. These are early, usually unedited copies of the book with plain bindings and without the finished cover. The reality of today's publishing is that it's sometimes easier to send finished books. However, major review journals insist on reviewing galleys, and won't review finished books. To get around the conundrum, you have two good choices: You can print up a few galleys, for the handful of reviewers who won't look at finished books, or you can mutilate finished books and pretend that they're advance galleys (rip off the covers, and replace with plain cardboard bindings). Your local copy shop can do either of these for you. Here's the information you should type on the front cover of the galley:

o The words "Uncorrected Proof," "Advance Review Copy," or "Pre-Publication Galley"

o Title, subtitle, and author of the book

o ISBN and categories (For example, this book's categories are Writing/Business.)

o Publisher name and contact information (address, telephone, website, email)

o Publication month (make this up, and set it at least three to six months from now to maximize your publicity and reviews). Include the month and year.

o Retail price, page count, trim size (the dimensions of the book—8.5 by 5.5, for example), binding (softcover or hardcover)

o Distribution (Ingram, Baker & Taylor, or any of the non-exclusive or exclusive distributors)

o Library cataloging numbers (CIP or PCN)

o Illustrations, index, appendices, or bibliography, if any

o Book Club rights, paperback rights, audio rights, movie rights, serial rights, foreign rights, or anything else of that ilk. Most publishers won't yet have this information.

o Size of print run (only include this if you're going to tell them *at least* 30,000)

o Author tour details—number of cities, amount of budget to be spent on the author tour. Include this only if 5 cities or more.

o Ad/promotion budget. Include this only if more than $30,000.

o Any advance quotes from reviewers

o Name (and contact info) of publicist who can be contacted for more details

• Along with the book itself, send the reviewers a cover letter. (You can sign it as the author or with the name of a "publicist" if you like). The letter should include all the details above, as well as a description of the contents, why the book is important, what the market is, and a little about the author's credentials, including previously published books.

- Be sure to mail all review copies USPS Priority Mail, FedEx or UPS overnight.

- Send your books to the following reviewers:

  o *Publishers Weekly*, 245 West 17th Street, New York, NY 10011, (212)463-6782, fax (212)463-6631, www.PublishersWeekly.reviewsnews.com/index.asp?layout=submissions

    Publishers Weekly reviews 5,000 books out of close to 50,000 submissions. Send galleys 3 months before publication date; they never review books after publication date. Their new submissions guidelines indicate that they *will* consider self-published books, if you "print at least 2,000 and have an arrangement with a reputable distributor." (But your chances of being reviewed are higher if you do not call yourself "self-published.")

  o *Library Journal*, Book Review Editor, 245 West 17th Street, New York, NY 10011, Toll-free (888)800-5473 or (212)463-6818, fax (212)463-6734, BkRev@LJ.Cahners.com, www.libraryjournal.com/about/submission.asp

Library Journal goes to over 28,000 librarians: 50% of them public libraries, 21% academic libraries, 13% special libraries, and 6% school libraries. They review 6,000 books out of 40,000 submissions. A good review in Library Journal, according to their own promotional material, will sell over 1,000 books; a rave review on a high-demand topic may move 5,000. Most of these library orders will come through a library wholesaler, and some 80% of these through Baker & Taylor. Send galleys 3-4 months before publication date.

o American Library Association *Booklist* Magazine, 50 East Huron Street, Chicago, IL 60611, (800)545-2433, fax (312)337-6787, www.ala.org/booklist, or email Bonnie Smothers at BSmothers@ala.org or Editor and Publisher Bill Ott at Bott@ala.org

Booklist reviews 4,000 adult books, 2,500 children's books, and 500 reference books each year. Send galleys 3-4 months before publication date.

   ▪ Adult books to Brad Hooper

   ▪ Children's books to Stephanie Zvirin

   ▪ Reference books to Mary Ellen Quinn

o *Foreword Magazine*, Alex Moore, Book Review Editor, 129½ East Front Street, Traverse City, MI 49684, (231)933-3699, fax (231)933-3899,

www.ForewordMagazine.com/reviews/re
vsguidelines.asp

Foreword reviews books from independent and university presses. Submit galleys and cover art 3-4 months before publication date. They review 600 books (out of 7,000 submitted) each year, 90% of which are nonfiction. Circulation is 20,000.

o *Kirkus Reviews*, 770 Broadway, New York, NY 10003, (212)777-4554, fax (212)979-1352, www.KirkusReviews.com

Send Kirkus *two* copies of galleys at least 3 months before publication date. They receive over 70,000 manuscripts.

- One caveat about Kirkus Reviews: Amazon now posts Kirkus Reviews at the very top of their listings—even above the book's basic description. That's great if you've garnered a fantastic review—and terrible if you have a lukewarm review.

o *Choice*, 100 Riverview Center, Middletown, CT 06457, (860)347-1387, fax (860)346-8586

Send only finished books appropriate to colleges and research libraries to Choice.

o Jim Cox, *Midwest Book Review*, 278 Orchard Drive, Oregon, WI 53575, (608)835-7937,

MBR@ExecPC.com,
www.MidwestBookReview.com

Send finished books only.

o *Fearless Book Reviews,* 1678 Shattuck Avenue #319, Berkeley, CA 94709, Queries@FearlessBooks.com

Send finished books only.

o *The New York Times Book Review,* 229 W. 43rd Street, New York, NY 10036, (212)556-7267

o *School Library Journal,* 245 W. 17th Street, New York, NY 10011, (212)463-6759

Send only books appropriate for K-12 school libraries.

• In addition to pursuing the biggest review journals, you might want to spend some time getting reviews from smaller publications. Reviews from groups respected by your niche market are much easier to come by than reviews in Publishers Weekly—and are more likely to sell books to readers in your niche. Check *The Encyclopedia of Associations, The Oxbridge Directory of Newsletters* and *Standard Rate and Data Services Business Publications* for outstanding lists of associations, varied newsletters, and trade publications respectively, for publications that might be interested in reviewing your book.

List with Wholesalers

Today, you'll also send your book to the wholesalers. Ingram and Baker & Taylor are the two essentials on this list: Together, they control most of the book sales to bookstores and libraries in the country. But you may also want to explore a myriad of smaller, non-exclusive and exclusive distributors. Details on these distributors, and explanations of the differences between wholesalers, exclusive distributors, non-exclusive distributors, and fulfillment houses, can be found in Appendix F: Wholesalers, Distributors and Fulfillment.

- There are two approaches to getting into the wholesalers. The first is to apply directly—and see if they say yes. The second is to generate demand for your books in bookstores and libraries—and then approach the wholesalers. The advantage of applying first is that when bookstores approach the wholesalers with a request for your book, you'll already be listed and won't lose those sales; the disadvantages are that if there's been no demand for your book the wholesalers may not jump for joy to add you to their database, and that they will levy a fee for your inclusion. (Baker & Taylor now charges $150 for new vendors.) (Comparatively, the advantage of first generating demand is that the wholesalers will be happy to include you and will not charge the fee; the disadvantage is that you may lose sales in the interim.) It can't hurt your chances to apply (and then follow the second approach if you are turned down.)

- Baker & Taylor will accept small publishers with only one or a few titles. Ingram, on the other hand, recently announced that they will no longer work with small independent publishers: Their recommendation is to get into the Ingram system via a relationship with Biblio, Lightning Source, or Xlibris (more information on these companies appears below.) There is, of course, a backdoor, if you're determined to work with Ingram directly: If you can prove you are generating enough national publicity, and that there is enough bookstore demand for your book, they will grudgingly let you into the club. In approaching Ingram, therefore, be certain you have as much ammunition as possible: National magazine exposure, BookSense selection, and review journals all work in your favor. When you contact them, send them the complete list of ISBNs and titles you're planning to carry—you don't have to tell them when—in order to appear large enough to be attractive.

  o **Ingram:** Publisher Relations Department, Ingram Distribution Group, One Ingram Boulevard, PO Box 3006, La Vergne, TN 37086, (615)287-5350 or (800)937-8000. Buyer@IngramBook.com

     For information on getting into Ingram through Biblio, Xlibris, or Lightning Source, see www.Ingrambook.com and select "Ingram Publisher Relations."

- o **Baker & Taylor,** 44 Kirby Avenue, PO Box 6885, Bridgewater, NJ 08807, (800)775-1100, fax (908)704-9460, PubSvc@BTol.com.

  Request their application for new publishers.

- For the latest wrinkles and challenges in being accepted by wholesalers, and to find out the latest methods around the system, join *Publishers Advocate* (www.PublishersAdvocate.com).

Day Number 3

Today you'll **generate quotations** which will be used in your publicity materials.

Generate Quotations

Quotations, also called blurbs, are included in all publicity materials and on or in the book itself to help make sales. Here are the details:

- Start by approaching people you know, or to whom you have some connection: Your mayor, your senators or congressmen, your tourist bureau or chamber of commerce, your local acquisitions librarian, your local independent or chain bookseller. Hand deliver your book to these people—and ask for their quotations in person.

- Continue by finding famous people who are most qualified or most appropriate to comment on your book. Check out www.experts.com and www.ProfNet.com for two good places to locate corporate figures, politicians, doctors, researchers, and others who might want to comment on your book (for publicity purposes of their own). ProfNet alone features over 15,000 self-proclaimed experts: Send email, with your specific expert request and deadline, to profnet@profnet.com.

- In addition to celebrities, politicians, and experts, consider getting quotations from corporate executives whom you might later want to approach about quantity sales of your book for their organization. It's a much easier sale to IBM if the CEO's laudatory comment is splashed across the cover of the book. (See the order form at the back of this book for our special report, *Sell Your Books to Corporations*.)

- A sure-fire way to generate great quotations for your book is to make your first contact by asking them for information on their organization, or advice or tips to include in the text of your book. Follow up with a thank you note for their information, and include a copy of your book or galley, with a request for a quotation. If you've mentioned the person or organization, be sure to write "You're featured on page. 270!" on the outside of the envelope. Since they've already contributed material to your book, they'll feel some sense of ownership of it, and will be predisposed to write you a good blurb. You may find it easiest to get the use of their name if you include a sample of the sort of quotation—or even the exact wording—that you'd like to use. (Since celebrities and politicians may be too busy to read your book, make it easy for them: Suggest the sort of quotation you have in mind and let them tinker with it. This will save them time, and give you exactly the sort of blurb you need!) Be sure to send your book or galley to them via USPS Priority Mail, FedEx, or UPS.)

- Finally, write thanking them for their quotation, and pointing out where it is featured ("As you can see, we were privileged to include your wonderful words on the back cover/in the front pages/on our publicity postcards…") and including a copy of the (signed) book as a thank you. At this time, it's appropriate to ask that if they know of anyone who might be interested in quantity purchases of the book, distributing it to employees or members of an organization, selling it on their website, etc, to please put them in touch. I shy away from asking most people if they want to purchase the book directly—but have no problem asking if they know of anyone *else* who might want the book.

- Once you have good quotations, where should you put them? Everywhere! Include them:
  - On your website
  - On the back cover of your book
  - In the front matter of your book
  - In the signature file of your email
  - On your Amazon and BN.com pages
  - On your postcards
  - In your press releases
  - In your letters to the media
  - At the bottom of invoices to wholesalers
  - In letters to readers who buy your book directly

Day Number 4

Today you'll **design and order postcards**.

Create Postcards

One of your most effective tools in the publishing game will be postcards featuring your book on one side, order information on the other side. You will mail these to reviewers, media, libraries, and bookstores. You will post them on lampposts and kiosks, and include them with every outgoing book order. You will pass them out at book shows and give them to your kids to hand out at the playground. And they're not very expensive—500 postcards cost just over $100, and 5,000 postcards cost under $500 to print. Here are some things to consider:

- Order your postcards early in the process. It may take several days to get them produced, and you want to get them in the mail as soon as possible.

- Don't order too many right away. You'll probably want to reprint them once you have some great quotations and reviews to include.

- There are several good postcard producers. Some of them will also do the mailing for you, if you supply them with a mailing list. Here are my favorites:

  o Modern Postcard, 1675 Faraday Avenue, Carlsbad, CA 92008, (800)959-8365,

customerservice@ModernPostcard.com,
www.modernpostcard.com

o Tu-Vets Printing, 5635 E. Beverly Blvd, Los
Angeles, CA 90022, (800)894-8977, Tu-
Vets@aol.com, www.tu-vets.com

o U.S. Press, 1628 James P. Rodgers Drive,
Valdosta, GA 31601, (800)227-7377,
www.uspress.com, (they don't accept email)

o 4by6.com offers good prices if you want
under 500 postcards. 527 23rdAvenue #120,
Oakland, CA 94606. (510)536-9565.
service@4by6.com, www.4by6.com

- On one side of the postcard put the front cover
art from your book.

- On the other side, include the title of your book;
a brief and catchy description; one or two of your
best quotations; the book's ISBN; the publishing
house name, contact address (regular and email),
and phone number for orders, particularly if you
have an 800 number; wholesalers who stock the
book (or exclusive distributor, if you have one);
page count, hardcover or paperback, and
(optional) retail price.

On my postcards, I run the copy down the left
side of the postcard, and draw the "middle" line
closer than the midway point to the right edge of
the postcard, because you won't need as much
space for the mailing label and stamp as you do

for everything you want to say about the book. If you're *positive* the postcards will only be included in other mailings—and never mailed directly—utilize the "address half" of the postcard as well. For example, here is the back of the postcard I used for my book *Terrorism and Kids: Comforting Your Child*:

Terrorism and Kids

Comforting Your Child

by Fern Reiss

The world today is a scary place. Will your child be ok? Symptoms to look for, strategies to employ, and answers to difficult questions children will ask.

"A wonderful resource and must-have for every parent & teacher." — Aviva Bock, psychotherapist and Harvard Medical School instructor.

"A compelling glimpse into today's world and America's newest challenge. Thank you. — Senator Edward Kennedy, Massachusetts.

ISBN 1-893290-09-3, 160 pages, ppb, $14.95. Available through Ingram, Baker & Taylor, and Quality Books. Or order directly from Peanut Butter and Jelly Press at www.TerrorismAndKids.com.

Peanut Butter and Jelly Press
PO Box 590239
Newton, MA 02459-0002
PBJPress.com

A Book Sense 76 Pick for January / February 2002

Bring "Terrorism and Kids" to your library! Author Fern Reiss speaks at libraries nationwide. Seminars include a lecture, popular question/answer session, and autographing. Usual fee is $500. Fern Reiss is an engaging and in-demand speaker. To book her for your library, contact Alyza@PBJPress.com.

(Note that this postcard was not intended to be mailed, and so it uses the address part of the right-hand side. Without that paragraph of text, though, it does follow U.S. Postal Service requirements.)

- Be aware that the U.S. Postal Service is very picky about postcards, including what size can be mailed at postcard rate. If your postcard is oversized, it will be charged first-class letter rate, rather than the less expensive postcard rate) and which "no-print" zones must be left blank for postal service use. Check with your postcard printer for current details.

- If you're planning or hoping to speak at libraries, schools, organizations, or bookstores—particularly if you have visions of a cross-country tour including lots of speeches—include that information on your postcard. I've spoken coast to coast about my books, and many of the librarians, corporations, adult education centers, and organizations have found me through my postcard mailings.

- If you're planning to sell special reports on your topic then include that information on the postcard, as well. (I know, I know, you haven't written the reports yet. Don't worry—just include the details. We'll get there soon.)

- If there's a particular niche or market to which your book will appeal, consider a postcard mailing to the members of that group: I mail *Publishing Game* postcards to writing organizations and writing conferences nationwide, for example.

- Mail your postcard to acquisitions librarians, schools, organizations, corporations, and booksellers across the country.

- Authors: Present your publisher with a plan of where you'd like to mail them, and see if your publisher will pick up the cost of your postcards.

(And the mailing—which can cost much more than printing the postcards!)

Day Number 5

Today you'll set up a **website** for your book.

Put Up a Website

This section won't provide comprehensive details on how to set up a website—that's far beyond the scope of this book, and you'll need a good web designer or web skills of your own. But here are some of the considerations:

- Even if you already have a website, consider setting up a separate website for the book, so that people can find it easily if they search for it. Start by settling on a domain name. (The one for this book is www.PublishingGame.com.) I recommend buying a unique name for each book. Although it's more expensive, it makes it much easier for people to remember how to find the book, because the book title and domain name are the same.

- Make sure your website is listed with search engines. You can do this yourself, by putting in meta-tags and submitting it yourself to the top dozen search engines. Or you can hire someone to do this for you.

- Take credit cards. People are much more likely to buy your book if they can buy it instantly, on line, without thinking twice. Studies show that sites with credit card capabilities garner more sales than sites without credit cards. Don't make it difficult for people to buy the book; get hooked up with a merchant account at a credit card company.

- Make sure you set up your site so that your readers can order more than one item. Right now you have one book: By the end of the month, you will have a series of special reports for sale as well, all of which will generate income.

- When you fill web orders (or direct orders that come in by phone or mail, as well) be sure to include a little something extra that the customer doesn't expect—a bonus special report, a tips pamphlet, or the equivalent. This makes—and keeps—loyal customers.

- Make sure you include some sort of mailing list, or way to harvest names. You will start a special interest weekly email newsletter later on, and you'll be prepared with the perfect list of interested names. And when you write your next book, if it's on the same, or a related topic, you'll have an in-house list of buyers who will be interested in it.

- Don't forget to generate an automatic letter that goes to people who order your book, thanking them for their order, and reminding them of the other products and services you offer. Include all the quotationss and reviews you've garnered.

- Authors: Whether or not your publisher will let you fill orders for the book yourself (check out the contract you signed) get your book a website and boost your publicity efforts. Put in chatty information about yourself—people love to know more about the authors they're reading.

- If you're giving away freebies of any sort at your site, be sure to list it at www.FreeShop.com.

- When you're satisfied with your site, submit it to the site listing services for added publicity. www.toocool.com, www.cool.infi.net, and www.WhatsNu.com are among the best.

- If you're setting up the website yourself, see the following sites for guidance:

  o The WebPage-O-Matic helps you build a professional website quickly, easily, and automatically. It creates, uploads, and even promotes your site. www.WebPageOMatic.com.

  o You can build your site using free site design templates from www.toolsforthe.net.

  o Free clip art is available at www.webdesign.about.com/compute/web design/mlibrary.htm and www.webclipart.about.com.

  o Yahoo! Store is an easy way to set up an online store without start-up costs or time commitments. You pay a flat fee per month and the price includes the registry of your store in their shopping search engine. The price for a store carrying fewer than 50 items is $100 per month. www.store.yahoo.com EBiz Builder (www.e-bizbuilder.com) offers similar services.

o Great tips on web design can be found at www.WebDesign.about.com.

o If you want to add discussion forums and other interactive features to your website, see www.BuildACommunity.com. For free listserve software, see www.bcentral.com/products/lb/defaul t.asp

• If you're willing to spend the additional money to have someone else handle many of the details of your website, consider the following:

o BookZone, www.BookZone.com Several authors and independent publishers report favorably on their services, and their hosting packages range in price, starting at single title listings for $109 per year through more comprehensive packages starting at $700 per year plus a $350 set up fee. Contact them at Bookzone@Bookzone.com. or (800)536-6162.

o Future Thru Group, www.FutureThru.com Also used and recommended by many independent publishers, they supply web instruction so you can easily maintain your own site. Their price of $950 includes web design and one year of complimentary hosting. Contact Eric Anderson at (740)501-1058.

- You can eliminate all of these chores by signing your book into an existing bookseller's website, and letting them do the order taking and credit card processing. There are several sites that will do this for you; their services and fees vary. My personal favorite is www.IndyBook.com. Bonnie Hayskar has set this up to be serious competition for the wholesalers, and it's worth hooking up with her. Listings are $20/year plus a 5-12% credit card processing fee, depending on volume. You can find out more about IndyBook.com by sending email to info@IndyBook.com.

This week you:

- Made sure you have the basic components your book needs—ISBN, ABI, EAN barcode, and CIP data

- Decided on a discount schedule and terms

- Sent your book for reviews

- Submitted your book to the wholesalers

- Got quotationss or blurbs

- Designed and ordered postcards

- Set up a website for the book

Congratulations! You've made a great start!

Week Number Two

CR EO

This week you'll:

- Sell serial rights to major magazines

- Initiate the BookSense process

- Submit your book to the chain stores

- List your book with Amazon and the other online booksellers

- Announce your book to the libraries

- Submit your book to Library Approval Plans

- Submit your book to the book clubs

- Create a contact list

Day Number 6

Today you'll begin selling **serial rights to major magazines.**

Publish in Major Magazines

One of the best ways to get an advance buzz going for a new book is by selling the serial rights to major magazines. That means you're giving the magazine the right to print selected portions of the book in their magazine; they pay for this privilege, and you generate invaluable publicity. Here's how:

- Compose a letter to the magazine, explaining why your book would be of interest to their readers, and why you are qualified to write it.

- Include the chapter or excerpt that you think would be particularly appropriate for their audience—and explain why. Include a complete table of contents or description of the rest of the book, and offer them their choice of selection if they would prefer.

- You can offer the same chapter to different magazines, as long as you explain that you're submitting it simultaneously to other publications. Or you can carve out different chapters for different magazines, and offer each publication exclusivity.

- Contact information for major magazines is available online or via directories at your local library.

- Authors: Be sure to tell the magazines if your book is published by a major publishing house—and be sure to clear it with your publisher first!

Day Number 7

Today you'll initiate the **BookSense** process and submit your book to the major **chain stores**.

Try for a BookSense Endorsement

BookSense is a program of the American Booksellers Association, the umbrella organization for independent (non-chain) bookstores across the country. If you can get your book chosen as a BookSense selection, you will achieve national publicity. Here's how:

- Send email to Carl Lennertz (Carl@Booksense.com) telling him the name of the book and author, ISBN, publishing house and contact information, web address and email address, a brief description of the book, and the number of books you are offering to send (free) to bookstores. Then sit back and wait for booksellers to write and ask you for their books.

- Be prepared to give away (at no charge) at least 25-50 copies of your book to booksellers nationwide interested in considering it for their store (and for a BookSense selection.)

- BookSense recently instituted a listings charge; you can ante up the $100, or pay only half price if you're a member of PMA.

- Authors: If you have a publisher, ask them if your book will be offered through BookSense. If the answer is no, then buy enough copies so that you can offer it yourself. If you're doing it this way, be sure to mention the name of the publisher in your announcement—but give *your* email address for the book requests.

- Once booksellers receive your book, they'll nominate it for the BookSense list—if they like it. Your goal is to get enough recommendations to propel you onto the BookSense recommended list—if possible, to make it into the top ten positions, which get a lot more publicity than the remainder of the list. Making it onto this list won't necessarily get you great sales— the independent bookstores are, well, independent, and unfortunately don't necessarily buy their own recommendations—but it will reap great publicity, and may get you play in Publishers Weekly and other desirable venues.

- Consider getting the *Independent Bookstore Publicity Kit*, which lists independent bookstores' contact information, including fax numbers and email addresses, for hundreds of independent bookstores. See the order form at the back of this book for more information.

Sell to Chain Stores

Today you'll also send your book to the major chain stores for consideration. Chain stores are an important part of your book sales—and if you have a polished book, an easy sale to make. Here's how:

- Compose a letter to the chain stores detailing why your book is unique and will sell. Include any trade reviews you've received, and author credentials.

- Call Books-A-Million—(205)956-4151—to find out which buyer specializes in your sort of title: They have a children's buyer, a reference buyer, etc. (Neither Borders nor Barnes and Noble will divulge the names of their buyers.) Address the letter directly to the buyer.

- Send the chain stores the letter, a finished copy of the book, or galleys and cover art. Chain store buying processes are long and cumbersome, and it may take a while for you to be listed.

  o The largest chain is Barnes & Noble. Contact Marcella Smith, Barnes & Noble Small Press Department, 122 Fifth Avenue, New York, NY 10011, (212)633-3300, fax (212)463-5677, www.BarnesandNobleinc.com.

  Barnes and Noble responds in 6-8 weeks. They will also tell you *why* they didn't accept your book if they decline it—in which case, you will craft a letter explaining why their reasoning is incorrect, and try again.

o The second largest chain, including Borders, Waldenbooks, and Brentanos, is the Borders Group. Contact Borders, New Vendor Acquisitions, 100 Phoenix Drive, Ann Arbor, MI 48108, (734)477-4000 or (734)477-1111, fax (734)477-1313.

Borders will send you a postcard telling you whether your book has been accepted, and from which wholesaler they will be buying it. They insist that all communication take place via mail (and don't disclose their buyer names, phone numbers, or emails, for that reason.)

o The third largest chain is Books-A-Million, including Books-A-Million and Wal-Mart. Books-A-Million currently features over 200 stores in 18 states, with its heaviest concentration in the southeast. Contact them at 402 Industrial Lane, Birmingham, AL 35211. (205)942-3737, fax (205)945-8586.

They get most of their books from wholesaler American Wholesale Book Company. AWBC doesn't seem to respond to mail communication, but you can write a letter addressed to the book buyer and fax it to (256)764-2511.

o In Canada, contact the chain Chapters, 90 Ronson Drive, Etobicoke, Ontario M9W 1C1, (416)243-3138, fax (416)243-8964.

Day Number 8

Today, you'll submit your book to the major **online bookstores**.

Be Listed in Online Bookstores

Now, list your books with the online stores, primarily the two gorillas, Amazon.com and BN.com. It's easier to arrange to have your book carried by the online bookstores than by anyone else. And once you *are* listed online, it may give you more ammunition to go to the chains and other outlets and say, "Look, I'm selling like hotcakes on Amazon—you need to buy my book too!" So whether you want to be carried online or not, view this step as just another push into *all* the retail markets. Here's how:

- To list with Amazon, here's what to do:

    o Go to the Books homepage.

    o Scroll down and select "Publishers Guide".

    o Select "Complete Instructions".

    o Fill out the editorial information online. Keep in mind that all consumers will see, for the most part, is your top two or three reviewer comments. So make them count: Put *everything* that's important up here. I recommend including your email address or website in this area—so that customers can contact you directly with questions (or orders.)

o If you need to correct anything, email book-typos@amazon.com.

o Next, send your book cover (not the whole book, just the cover to be scanned) to:

> Amazon.com Advantage—Books
> PO Box 80727
> Seattle, WA 98108-0727

o Send a review copy of the book to Amazon Editors at PO Box 81226, Seattle, WA 98108, (800)570-1454. Include a letter explaining why they should review your title.

o Before you leave Amazon, do one more thing: Write a short and pithy review of at least one or two of Amazon's books that are similar to your book. Don't forget to sign off by mentioning the name of your book! (You can even include your email or web address—and send Amazon customers directly back to your site!)

o Amazon also offers a variety of merchandising options for independent publishers, with prices ranging from $500 to $9,000. For more details contact Lisa Biernbaum, Merchandising Manager, 705 5th Avenue South, Seattle, WA 98104, LBiern@Amazon.com. Questions about merchandising invoicing should go to Ki Cho at KCho@Amazon.com, (206)266-6763.

- To list with BN.com, here's what to do:

  o Go to the bottom of the www.BarnesAndNoble.com screen and select "Publishers and Authors Guide".

  o Click on "Establishing a Warehouse Relationship".

  o Fill out the publisher information form.

  o Then go back and read "How to submit content" and "How to sell us your new books".

  o BN.com will contact you within a few weeks.

  o Send any corrections (include title and ISBN) to corrections@barnesandnoble.com.

- To list with Books-A-Million, here's what to do:

  o Go to www.BAMM.com.

  o At the bottom of the screen select "For Publishers" and follow the directions. (Do not select "Pub Center" which is Books-A-Million's i-Universe pay-to-publish-online equivalent.)

Day Number 9

Today you'll announce your book to **libraries** and submit your book to **library approval plans**.

Sell to Libraries

There are over 15,000 public libraries in the U.S., as well as school libraries, university libraries, corporate libraries, and special libraries. If you sell your book to libraries, you can be a bestseller *just from your library sales alone.* Here's how to announce your title to libraries:

- Do a mailing to libraries. Both PMA and Sam Decalo at Florida Academic Press offer low-cost flyer mailings to libraries nationwide. Contact them for details:

  o Publishers Marketing Association, 627 Aviation Way, Manhattan Beach, CA 90266, (310)372-2732; fax (310)374-3342, PMAOnline@aol.com, www.PMA-Online.org

  o Sam Decalo, Florida Academic Press, PO Box 540, Gainesville, FL 32602. (352)332-5104. FAPress@worldnet.att.net

  o Or you can purchase a mailing list and do the mailing yourself. You can get top-notch lists from the following sources:

    ▪ Bowker (800)337-7184

- American Library Association (800)545-2433

- Library Journal (212)463-6819

- Booklist (312)944-6780

• Announce your book easily to hundreds of acquisitions libraries nationwide for only $1 per word. See www.PublishersAdvocate.com or the order form at the back of this book for details.

• Send your terms letter to the major library wholesalers so that they know where to find you when they receive orders for your book. You must apply for inclusion in Quality Book's program, because they actually have a sales force that markets your book to the libraries. The other library wholesalers simply fill library orders; don't bother sending them anything except your statement of terms.

   o Quality Books, 1003 West Pines Road, Oregon, IL   61061, (815)732-4450, fax (815)732-4499, Carolyn.Olson@Dawson.com

   o Brodart, 500 Arch Street, Williamsport, PA 17705. (800)233-8467

   o Academic Book Center, 5600 NE Hassalo Street, Portland, OR   97213, (503)287-6657, fax   (503)284-8859,   info@acbc.com, www.acbc.com

- o Emery Pratt, 1966 W. Main Street, Owosso, MI 48867, (517)723-5291, fax (517)723-4677

- o Midwest Library Service, 11443 St. Charles Rock Road, Bridgeton, MO 63044, (314)739-3100

Be Included in Library Approval Plans

Library approval plans are a way to get thousands of libraries to buy your book—automatically. Here's how it works: Many libraries today don't make their own acquisition selections, or at least don't make all of them. Instead they subscribe to a Library Approval Plan which sends them a selection of books, targeted for the constituents of the particular library. The upside for the library is better discounts; the program also frees up the personnel budget which would otherwise be spent on an acquisitions librarian (the funds for which can then be spent on books or other programs.) The downside, of course, is that it cuts out many independent publishers, who may find it difficult to get into this program (not to a small extent because they've never heard of it.) However, if you're got good reviews from the major journals, you can get in. Here's how:

- • The two largest—and most important—of the library approval plans are those coordinated by Yankee Book Peddler and Blackwell's/Academic Book Center.

- • Yankee Book Peddler takes its inventory from Baker & Taylor. You must be registered with Baker & Taylor to get into Yankee Book Peddler (but they don't take all books that Baker & Taylor carry.) YBP's market is exclusively college and university libraries, so only presses with a focus on the academic market will be accepted (though their definition of academic is fairly loose). In addition, YBP only accepts presses that produce *at least ten such titles per year.* Their core subject areas include the following:

o   Art, architecture, photography

o   Business, economics, and management

o   Education

o   Fiction and poetry

o   Gender Studies

o   Humanities

o   Law and criminology

o   Library science and reference publishing

o   Medicine, psychiatry, and health sciences

o   Multicultural topics

o   Museums and galleries

o   Music

o   Religion and theology

o   Science, technology, and computers

o   Social sciences

- Blackwell/Academic Book Center is not any more interested in small presses than YBP, and is even harder to contact except via mail. They also only accept academic presses doing more than a certain number of titles per year.

- If your press is ineligible, you can still get into the system through the backdoor: Persuade a local librarian to request your book from YBP or ABC directly. That will force your book into the database, which will then permit other libraries to get it that way. In addition, write to both companies and tell them the details of your book—author, ISBN, price—and include information on good reviews you've gotten, particularly from library journals. Then ask to be put on the list.

  o Yankee Book Peddler, 999 Maple Street, Contoocook, NH 03229, (800)258-3774, fax (603)746-5628,   service@ybp.com, www.ybp.com

  o Academic Book Center, 5600 NE Hassalo Street, Portland, OR 97213, (503)287-6657, fax   (503)284-8859,   info@acbc.com, www.acbc.com

Day Number 10

Today you'll submit your book to **book clubs**, create a **contact list**, and catch up on **loose ends**.

Sell to Book Clubs

Today you'll send the galleys of your book to book clubs. Here's how:

- Write a letter—by now you should be good at this—explaining why your book is important, who the audience is, and why the author is qualified to write it (see example on next page).

- Include your publishing house contact information and any advance reviews or quotes.

- Do not send finished books, even if you have them. Send galleys. Book clubs like to think they've got the book months before everyone else.

- Book clubs require a several month lead time. So give them a publication date that sounds very far away.

Peanut Butter and Jelly Press LLC, PO Box 590239, Newton, MA 02459 (617)630-0945 phone/fax
info@PBJPress.com ᔕ "Extraordinary books on everyday topics" ᔕ www.PBJPress.com

September 3, 2002

Dear Book Club Editor,

Anyone can create a bestseller.

It takes time. It takes energy. It takes motivation and passion.
Most authors have all that.

What they don't usually have is a *plan*.

Every long-range goal requires a plan. If you're going to
compete in a marathon, you make up a training schedule. If
you decide to apply to graduate school, you make up a list of
requirements. If you want to lose weight, you follow a diet.

If you want to create a bestseller, you need a day-by-day plan so you know where you're
heading, and what you need to do each day to get there.

The Publishing Game: Bestseller in 30 Days is that plan. Whether you're an author or a
small publisher, it will take you step-by-step and day-by-day through the hoops necessary to
make your book a bestseller.

Fern Reiss is the author of several award-winning and best-selling books, including the
recently acclaimed **Terrorism and Kids: Comforting Your Child**. Here she shares the
secrets to bestselling success—and the day by day steps necessary to make *any* non-fiction
book a bestseller.

We enclose an advance unedited galley of the manuscript, along with a rough mockup of the
planned cover. Please let us know if you'd be interested in **The Publishing Game:
Bestseller in 30 Days** for Writer's Digest Book Club. The book's publication date is
scheduled for October 2002.

Sincerely,

Alyza Harris
Peanut Butter and Jelly Press

- All the major book clubs are now under the aegis of BookSpan. Below is contact information for the four largest book clubs:

  o Book of the Month Club, Time & Life Building, 1271 Avenue of the Americas, 3rd floor, New York, NY 10020, (212)522-4200

  o Quality Paperback Book Club, Time & Life Building, 1271 Avenue of the Americas, 3rd floor, New York, NY 10020, (212)522-5674, fax (212)522-0303

  o Doubleday, Time & Life Building, 1271 Avenue of the Americas, 3rd floor, New York, NY 10020, (212)522-4200

  o Literary Guild, Time & Life Building, 1271 Avenue of the Americas, 3rd floor, New York, NY 10020, (212)522-8051, fax (212)522-0303

- See the www.booksonline.com site for over 20 additional book clubs that might be appropriate for your particular book. Then send your book, addressed to the book club, at the following address:

  Bookspan
  1271 Avenue of the Americas, 3rd floor
  New York, NY 10020
  (212)522-4200.

- Book clubs pay, on average, $5000 for a main selection, much less for an alternate selection. But it's great publicity.

Make a Contact List

Now begin putting together a running list of contacts. These include your wholesalers, distributors, chain bookstores, online bookstores, press contacts, people who gave you quotations, librarians, independent booksellers, etc. You'll add to this list every time you make a new contact—and fax or email them every other week, to make sure they remember your name, and the name of your book. This gets the buzz going.

Tie Up Loose Ends

- Follow up with the celebrities, politicians, and experts from whom you're expecting blurbs.

- Email Reviews@ForewordMagazine.com to ensure that they received your review copy.

- Email LJQuery@Cahners.com to ensure that Library Journal received your review copy.

- Send a copy of the printed book to the CIP office, for final cataloging: 101 Independence Avenue SE, Washington, DC 20540.

This week you:

- Sold serial rights to major magazines
- Initiated the BookSense process
- Submitted your book to the chain stores
- Listed your book with Amazon and the other online booksellers
- Announced your book to the libraries
- Submitted your book to Library Approval Plans
- Submitted your book to book clubs
- Created a contact list

Congratulations! Your book is on its way!

Week Number Three

∽ ∾

This week you'll:

- Begin a print media publicity campaign
- Begin a broadcast media publicity campaign
- Offer a talk to local libraries, bookstores, and adult education centers
- Sell short selections to major magazines
- Participate in The Great Library Experiment
- Enter a contest
- Remember to email or fax your contact list and update your progress chart

Day Number 11

Today you'll orchestrate a **print media publicity campaign**.

Do a Print Media Publicity Campaign

Today you'll orchestrate a print media publicity campaign. There are three possible tactics to use:

- Do it all yourself.

    o Begin by writing and typesetting a press release and a review of your book, including a photo of the cover. Many publications, particularly newspapers, will print these directly, verbatim. Be sure to include ordering information, particularly your toll-free order number and website.

    o Distribute this press release and review to all the major print media. You can find lists of addresses in *Bacon's Directory* which is available at most public libraries.

    o Post your press release or review to all the free press release services online. Since they're free, all you have to lose is the few minutes it takes you to post. And web experts claim that even the sites that don't generate too much media attention are useful because they provide a free link to your website, which draws search engine traffic. Here are some of the best free press release services; you can find dozens more by searching online:

- www.PRWeb.com

- www.PressBox.co.uk

- www.solonews.com

- www.eBookBroadcast.com (on new e-books and e-publishing topics only)

o Don't forget that there are entrees into print media other than reviews. Propose (or simply write and submit) an article, list of tips, or opinion piece on your book's topic. The trick in dealing with the media—at least at the beginning—is to aim at the smaller slower targets, and wait for the larger targets to come to you. Everyone ignores this advice: Unknown authors send their manuscripts to Ladies Home Journal and Redbook; small publishers contact Oprah and Rosie. But the truth is, whatever media you're trying to break into, it's much, *much* easier to break in if you start small. Contact weekly newspapers rather than dailies; regional newsletters rather than nationals. Check out *Working Press of the Nation* for internal employee newsletters to target.

o Don't forget the less obvious places—your alumni magazine, your hometown newspaper, your *parents'* hometown newspaper, your synagogue or church publication, and newsletters of trade associations to which you belong.

- Do some of it yourself.

  o Start by paying someone to write a terrific press release for your book. My favorite is Shel Horowitz, whose charge for a great press release is $100-$250. Contact Shel Horowitz at Accurate Writing & More, PO Box 1164, Northampton, MA   01061, (413)586-2388, Shel@FrugalFun.com, www.frugalmarketing.com.

  o Then use a fax service to transmit it to as many newspapers and magazines as you can afford. Paul Krupin's excellent fax service charges $ 0.25 per fax, with a $50 minimum, and he'll custom design a targeted list for your book.   Contact Paul at (800)457-8746. info@IMediaFax.com.

- The third option is to use a public relations agency. If you're not interested in pursuing a publicity campaign on your own—and many people aren't—tap the services of one of the many wonderful book PR agents across the country. There are small agencies and big agencies, a la carte services and package plans. There's something to suit every taste—and almost every budget. Here are just a few options:

  o Stacey J. Miller of Randolph, Massachusetts offers a variety of high-quality services, including press kits ($300) and "eblasts" for $399. Total packages start at $700. She also offers book tours, radio blitzes, reviews, and other more traditional PR opportunities. S.J. Miller Communications, 10 Turning Mill Lane, Randolph, MA 02368, (888)777-0884, fax (781)963-68883, SJMiller@BookPR.com, www.BookPR.com and www.OnlineBookPR.com

o Marcia Yudkin offers a variety of unusual publicity plans, including $1000 to become a respected name in any industry, to $2000 for a complete product or service marketing makeover. She also offers press releases and sales letter makeovers for $100-200. Contact: Marcia Yudkin, PO Box 1310, Boston, MA 02117, (617)266-1613, fax (781)647-9426, Marcia@Yudkin.com, www.Yudkin.com/consulting.htm.

o Kate Bandos offers various PR services, including a very attractive a la carte menu with prices starting as low as $5 per contact. KSB Promotions, 55 Honey Creek Ave NE, Ada, MI 49301, (616)676-0758, PR@KSBPromotions.com

o Bev Harris of Talion offers a range of PR options starting at $349 and going on into the stratosphere. Talion.com, 330 SW 43rd Street, PMB K-547, Renton, WA 98055. (425)228-7131, fax (425)228-3965. feedback@talion.com, www.talion.com

o Tami DePalma and Kim Dushinski at Marketability offer expensive but high quality PR services for small publishers. Full PR campaign prices begin at $5000. Kim or Tami@Marketability.com

o Claire Kirch is more in touch with the independent bookstore scene than most publicists, because she also edits a book review newsletter for the independents. Her services include advance comments, press kits, media followup, author tours, and more, for $80/hour. Contact her at: Claire Kirch Publicity Services, 8 North Second Avenue East #306, Duluth, MN 55802, (218)727-8373, ClaireKirch@aol.com.

o See also the listings under Broadcast Publicity Campaigns (day number 12); many publicists do both print and broadcast publicity.

Day Number 12

Today you'll initiate your **broadcast media campaign**.

Do a Broadcast Media Campaign

As with the print media, it's much harder to hit the major television shows than the small ones. Instead of spending a lot of energy trying to crack Oprah, focus your time and attention on the hundreds of smaller shows. It's certainly easier to get yourself booked—and you may find that you sell just as many books that way. Here's how to begin:

- You'll need three things to hit the major broadcast media: Media savvy (there are all kinds of special tips on getting on to big radio and TV shows, and what to do once you're there); a good hook in a good letter that you can email or fax to producers; and a list of whom to contact.

  - There are literally hundreds of people who claim to be able to train you in pitching yourself to the broadcast media, or in the art of media coaching, as it's known. The best in the business is Joel Roberts, and his coaching (which is available privately by telephone, or as an in-person weekend conference with a group of other authors and speakers in locations across the country) is among the best, as well as most reasonably priced; his two-day media seminar is $995. Joel is also a frequent and popular speaker at national speaking and independent publishing conferences. Contact him at: Joel Roberts, 2263 Fox Hills Drive #302, Los Angeles, CA 90064, (310)286-0631, fax (310)785-0439, JDRob36@aol.com.

o On the next page there is a sample of the sort of hook that attracts the broadcast media— but my advice is to invest in a weekend with Joel and have him help you craft your own letter.

o Along with your letter, include a list of at least ten provocative, interesting questions that you can answer on the air. Here's a surprise: The point here is *not* to talk about your book. The point is to say interesting things on a topic related to your book. Don't worry: The interviewer will mention your book several times. But the easiest way to get on the air is if you can be witty, warm, irreverent or provocative—on any topic.

Peanut Butter and Jelly Press LLC, PO Box 590239, Newton, MA 02459 (617)630-0945 phone/fax
info@PBJPress.com ✆ "Extraordinary books on everyday topics" ✆ www.PBJPress.com

September 3, 2001

Dear _____,

Today, Fern Reiss and her husband happily enjoy their three
children. But for three years, they, like 25 million Americans,
experienced the anguish of infertility and miscarriage.

Until they changed, of all things, their diets—and conceived in
two months. Yes, it was *what they ate—and didn't eat*—that turned
out to be the key to getting pregnant.

And even though Fern's recently published book, *The Infertility
Diet: Get Pregnant and Prevent Miscarriage*, is based on 500 medical
studies that show a link between food and fertility, doctors are
unlikely to suggest nutritional changes for infertility—because
there's no money in yams and pumpkin seeds. Fern Reiss is no doctor, though she's read
hundreds of medical studies. What she is—now—is a mother.

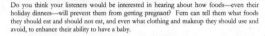

Do you think your listeners would be interested in hearing about how foods—even their
holiday dinners—will prevent them from getting pregnant? Fern can tell them what foods
they should eat and should not eat, and even what clothing and makeup they should use and
avoid, to enhance their ability to have a baby.

Fern is a compelling interview, and has been a frequent radio and television guest (She just
appeared on national Fox-TV News).

I look forward to speaking to you about Fern Reiss soon.

Sincerely,

Alyza Harris
Peanut Butter and Jelly Press

○ There are several companies that provide contact information on the broadcast media, and many that also enable you to pitch yourself to the producers directly (or do it for you.) Here is a sampling:

- Radio-TV Interview Report is the largest and most visible player in this area, producing a weekly print newsletter that goes to thousands of television and radio producers nationwide. Ads here are steep—a half page, for example, will run $500, with discounts for quantity purchases. People have reported varying success. The editors at this publication are top-notch—and it might be worth buying one ad simply for the service (included at no additional charge) of having their people rewrite your publicity release. (Or you can ask for a few free back issues and read enough samples to figure out how to craft this sort of intriguing pitch yourself.) Bradley Communications, 135 East Plumstead Avenue, Landsdowne, PA 19050, (800)553-8002, fax (610)259-5032, ContactUs@RTIR.com, www.RTIR.com

- Yearbook of Experts' RadioTour.com offers packages that include audio message listings going to 1,000 shows and email announcements going to more. $500 buys 90 days of audio releases. (202)333-4904, RadioTour.com

- Lorilyn Bailey's Guestfinder.com lists and promotes aspiring media guests. Prices start at $250/year. PO Box 40304, Raleigh, NC 27629, (919)878-9108, info@GuestFinder.com or LorilynB@ral.mindspring.com

- If you have the budget for it, Rick Frishman, president of Planned Television Arts, one of the premier media placement services in the country, says that a typical low-end campaign of morning drive radio shows runs $4000. A mid-level campaign, adding print and some nationals, runs $20,000; and a high-end, adding satellite television and 5-10 city tours runs closer to $50,000. More information is available at www.PlannedTVArts.com.

- See also the listings under Print Publicity Campaigns (day number 11); many publicists do both print and broadcast publicity.

o Don't forget: Before the show, notify local bookstores so they can get in a supply of your books. Be sure to send the host of the show an (autographed) copy of your book, along with a list of sample questions (to which you've already crafted great answers!) Remember when you're on the show to ask listeners to get a pen so that you can give them some special tidbit or tip—and with the tip, repeat your web address or order number, so they'll be able to write it down.

o   Be sure to have a professional videotape made of your television appearances. All the big shows—including Oprah—will ask for this tape when they're considering you for an appearance. Here is a company with offices in every major metropolitan area that provides this service:

- Video Monitoring Services of America, 330 West 42nd Street, New York, NY 10036, (212)736-2010, fax (212)736-8206, NYSales@vmsinfo.com, www.vms.com

Day Number 13

Today you'll offer a **local talk**, and sell short selections of your book to **major magazines**.

Offer to Speak Locally

Libraries, bookstores, and adult education centers are constantly looking for good speakers, and authors are among their favorites. Don't overlook this as an income opportunity, either. Although bookstores don't generally pay for talks, and adult education centers pay minimally, libraries often have good budgets—and good speakers, with good books, can command high prices. (Actually, even highly mediocre speakers can be well paid for talks, as long as the talk is in demand.) Here are some tips:

- You can announce your talk to several hundred librarians, adult education center directors, and booksellers, via the *Publishers Advocate* email newsletter. See the Publishers Advocate appendix or PublishersAdvocate.com for more details.

- Or contact the bookstores yourself: Our *Independent Bookstore Publicity Kit* contains fax numbers and email addresses for hundreds of independent bookstores nationwide; see the order form at the back of this book for more information.

- Contact local chain stores. The more feedback the national buyers get from the regional stores, and the more books you can successfully push through the local stores, the more ammunition you have in making a case for your book on the national level. So give some talks at your local chain stores, and see whether you can get some good referrals to propel you into the national league.

Sell to Major Magazines

Today you'll also begin selling short excerpts from your book to national magazines. Small tidbits from your book are easy to sell to major magazines. Here's how:

- Sit down right now and make a list of something from your book—such as, "Ten Foods to Lose Five Pounds Today" or "Six Tips for Getting Started in Homeschooling."

- Keep it to one or two typed pages. Be sure to double space between lines.

- Include information on how readers can get the whole book, including your website and order phone number.

- Then send it to any of the following publications that are appropriate:

  o Bottom Line, 55 Railroad Avenue, Greenwich, CT 06830

  o Family Circle, Circle, 375 Lexington Avenue, 9th floor, New York, NY 10017

- o Good Housekeeping, 959 Eighth Avenue, New York, NY 10019

- o Ladies Home Journal, 125 Park Avenue, 20th floor, New York, NY 10017

- o Newsweek, 251 West 57th Street, New York, NY 10019

- o The New York Times, 229 West 43rd Street, New York, NY 10036

- o Parade Magazine, 711 Third Avenue, New York, NY 10017

- o Redbook Magazine, 224 West 57th Street, 6th floor, New York, NY 10019

- o Time Magazine, Time-Life Building, Rockefeller Center, New York, NY 10020

- o USA Today, 1000 Wilson Boulevard, Arlington, VA 22229

- o Woman's Day, 1633 Broadway, 42nd floor, New York, NY 10019

Day Number 14

Today you'll participate in **The Great Library Experiment**.

Try The Great Library Experiment

The Great Library Experiment was designed as a way of increasing visibility of unknown author and independent press titles. Not so incidentally, it will also promote library sales of your book. Here's how to get started. Send the letter on the next page to ten friends.

More about The Great Library Experiment:

- Libraries base buying decisions on good reviews and customer requests. It may be too late to do anything about the reviews, but it's never too late to stimulate customer requests. Participating in The Great Library Experiment is one way to generate library purchases—because people all across the country will be requesting your book from their local library.

- Send the announcement to all your friends and relatives, or post it on your website and to your favorite writing and publishing lists, so others will send it around too. The more the list is circulated, the better everyone's books should do.

- Or start your own great library experiment—you're only as limited as your imagination!

- Look for updates on the success of the Great Library Experiment at www.PublishingGame.com.

Dear Friends,

Please help me out by participating in the Great Library Experiment! Here's how to play:

1. Go to your local library and request the number one book on the list below. If they don't have the book, then ask if they can please buy it for the library. When they get the book for you, read it. If you like it, make it a point to tell people about it. Review it on Amazon, encourage your book group to read it, or write a letter to the editor of your local newspaper. Email your friends about it. Help to spread the word!

2. Delete the number one book on the list below.

3. Add a book to the bottom of the list. If you're an author or independent publisher, add your own book. If you're not, just add your favorite (not yet popular) book. Include the ISBN and a tiny library review, if you like.

4. Send this entire message onward to ten (or more!) friends. If you're online, send it to your favorite lists and places where writers and publishers congregate.

That's it. Please don't try to cheat by putting your book on the top of this list. (If you do, only your ten friends will request your book--see? The only way to get a lot of people to hear about your book is to play by the rules.) And please don't break the chain!

If you'd like to find out whether this experiment worked or not, please check in at www.PublishingGame.com and we'll post the results as we get them. (You can also find an online version of the letter there, if it's easier for you to email it to friends.)

Thank you for participating in this experiment (which, by the way, is highly legal--I checked with an attorney just to be sure.) If you'd like to be informed of the next great experiment, send email to Experiment@PublishingGame.com. And thanks for playing!

The Great Library Experiment List of Books:

1. The Publishing Game: Publish a Book in 30 Days by Fern Reiss. ISBN 1-893290-85-9. $19.95.

2. The Publishing Game: Find an Agent in 30 Days by Fern Reiss. ISBN 1-893290-83-2. $19.95.

3. The Publishing Game: Bestseller in 30 Days by Fern Reiss. ISBN 1-893290-88-3. $19.95.

- Fax the media! If nothing else is new, announce your book's participation in the Great Library Experiment. The media are hungry for stories—it's your responsibility to keep them fed!

Day Number 15

Today you'll **enter a contest** and catch up on **loose ends**.

Enter a Contest

Submit your book for consideration to one or more of the following contests. They all cost money to enter, but the payoffs can be worthwhile. People are much more likely to buy a book that has received an award—even if it's an award they've never heard of. The following are all contests that you should consider:

- Benjamin Franklin Awards: Publishers Marketing Association organizes these annual awards. The cost is $60 per title for members. More information from Publishers Marketing Association, 627 Aviation Way, Manhattan Beach, CA 90266, (310)372-2732, fax (310)374-3342, www.pma-online.org, PMAOnline@aol.com.

- Independent Publisher Awards: 400 W. Front Street, Traverse City, MI 49684, (231)933-0445. Cost is $60 per title. More information is at www.IndependentPublisher.com.

- Foreword Magazine Awards: Cost is $50 per title. More information at *Foreword Magazine*, 129½ East Front Street, Traverse City, MI 49684, (231)933-3699, fax (231)933-3899, www.ForewordMagazine.com.

- Publishers Advocate Awards: Cost is $35. These are the only publishing awards given on an ongoing, rolling basis, so enter anytime during the year. (You must be a member of Publishers Advocate: Membership is $50 per year.) Send your galleys or printed book to Publishers Advocate Awards, PO Box 590239, Newton, MA 02459. You'll be notified as soon as your book has been evaluated. Include an additional $10 processing fee (and mark the package "Rush!") if you need to be notified in 10 days. If you meet the criteria—a professional cover including ISBN and bar code (if you're not sending a finished book include the name and email address of your cover artist), nice interior, carefully edited manuscript and good treatment of subject—you will be the recipient of a Publishers Advocate award. (Then ask your cover artist to incorporate the award logo into your cover design, or add the bright stickers to the front of your book.)

- Reading Group Choices: Cost is $700, but you only pay if you're accepted to be included in their annual directory that goes to 25,000 libraries, bookstores, and community book festivals nationwide. This may be worth considering for fiction or biographies. They charge stores for each copy of this directory, so presumably these aren't just being discarded. Reading Group Choices, 2106 Twentieth Avenue South, Nashville, TN 37212, (800)260-8605 or (615)298-2303, fax (615)298-9864. www.PazBookBiz.com, MKaufman@PazBookBiz.com.

- Consider awards specific to your book. If you're marketing a children's book, for example, consider the Parents Choice awards.

- Consider entering the Discover Great New Writers Program: Barnes & Noble sponsors this contest, aimed at fiction writers, four times a year. Send three galleys, cover art, author bio, and publicity information to Kelle Ruden, (212)633-3511, 122 Fifth Avenue, New York, NY 10011.

- Or create an award program of your own. I created one called the "I Love My Independent Bookstore Because..." contest (aimed at buyers patronizing independent bookstores) as a way of increasing the visibility of my publishing house, Peanut Butter and Jelly Press, to independent bookstores. For a minimal cost—in my case, $50 a month in prize money to the monthly contest winner—I got my name in front of the media and the book world, and most particularly the independent bookstores, for a full year. (The contest didn't hurt my book sales either—since a graphic of my book covers appeared on the very bottom of the poster announcing the contest.)

Tie Up Loose Ends

- Follow up with the responses you've gotten from BookSense stores. Send individual email responses to each bookseller who has requested the book informing them that the book is coming, telling them a bit more about it, and thanking them again for their interest. (Remind them, gently, that if they like the book they should please consider nominating you for a BookSense selection.) Then Priority Mail them the books!

- Once you've received requests for and mailed several books, compile all the emails addresses together (this is key--even the independents like to know they have company in thinking something's good) and mail to them thanking them for their interest and just checking to make sure they've received the book.

- If you have the time, and if it's appropriate for the book, sign your BookSense books before you ship them. Put an 'autographed by author' sticker on the cover. This makes it more valuable and personal to the booksellers.

- Follow up by telephone or email to make sure the chain bookstores have received your galleys.

- Follow up with the book clubs to whom you sent the bound galleys. By now you should have blurbs and reviews coming in—so be sure to mention that when you call to check on your progress. "I'm just calling to find out whether you'd reached a decision on making *Terrorism and Kids: Comforting Your Child* available to your readers—and wanted to make sure you knew it was just selected as a BookSense pick and endorsed by Senator Edward Kennedy."

- Remember to email or fax your contact list with the latest information on your book.   Update your progress chart.

- Email Publishers Weekly to be sure they've received your galley.   Identify the title, genre, publication month, author, publisher, and date sent.   They will respond only if they have *not* received the book. Email PWReviewStatus@cahners.com.

This week you:

- Began a print media publicity campaign
- Began a broadcast media publicity campaign
- Offered a talk to local libraries, bookstores, and adult education centers
- Sold short selections of your book to major magazines
- Participated in The Great Library Experiment
- Entered a contest
- Remembered to email or fax your contact list and updated your progress chart

Congratulations! You're building momentum!

Week Number Four

Cʒ ℰↃ

This week you'll:

- Create a holiday

- Submit a news story to a regional Publishers Weekly reporter

- Start working on quantity sales to organizations and corporations

- Sign up with a journalist referral service or as an online expert

- Send review copies to top Amazon reviewers

- Join a professional association

- Begin book sales to catalogs

- Remember to email or fax your contact list and update your progress chart

Day Number 16

Today you'll **create a holiday** and submit some news to your regional **Publishers Weekly** reporter.

Create a Holiday

Create a national holiday around your book. Anyone can create a national holiday—current listings in America include holidays such as "Fish Amnesty Day" and "National Tie Month." In 1994, Congress stopped recognizing special days sponsored by organizations and individuals, but there are two major services that now keep track of these new American holidays.

So think of a holiday that relates in some way to your book. The sky's the limit here. You can go serious or funny; heartwarming or hysterical. Think of something that is sure to draw media attention. Play around with this and bounce it off friends and relatives until you have something you're happy with. (Then write your press release announcing the holiday to the media. Just the process of writing the press release may alert you to details you'd like to include.)

List your holiday—with complete contact information for you and your publishing house—with these registries for free. Submit information on your holiday to:

- Chase's Calendar of Events, Contemporary Books, 4255 W. Touhy Avenue, Lincolnwood, IL 60646. (847)679-5500, fax (847)679-6358, www.Chases.com.

- The National Special Events Registry, Open Horizons, PO Box 205, Fairfield, IA   52556, `JohnKremer@BookMarket.com`.

- Submit the following information to both services:

  o Name of special day, week, month, or event

  o Date of event

  o Location of event

  o Estimated attendance

  o Sponsor's name, address, phone, fax, email and website

  o Short description of day or event

- All it takes is one tip-off to the media to alert them to your new holiday. If it's fun, funny, heartwarming, or interesting—you've just won yourself a load of free publicity for the two minutes it takes to fill out the form.

Submit a News Story to Regional PW

Publishers Weekly employs regional reporters whose job it is to report on the local publishing news. Today, figure out a local angle about your book—perhaps the holiday you've just created, or an interesting local reaction to the book—and call or email your local Publishers Weekly reporter to try to drum up an article. Be sure that you're calling them with a *news story*—the fact that you've written or published a book doesn't count as news, you need a hook that's real news. Once you come up with an angle, here's who to contact:

- New England: Judith Rosen, 196 Larch Road, Cambridge, MA 02138, (617)876-2469, fax (617)354-4811, Judith@twodogs.net

- West Coast: Bridget Kinsella, 479 Merritt Avenue Suite F, Oakland, CA 94610. (510)465-3853, BKinsella@cahners.com.

- Midwest: Brad Zellar, 4812 Chowen Avenue S., Minneapolis, MN 55410, (612)925-8616, Zellar@northwired.com.

- South: Bob Summer, PO Box 22392, Nashville, TN 37202, (615)352-4473, fax (615)256-4105, BSummer@dellnet.com.

- Canada: Leah Eichler, 150 Hilton Avenue #4, Toronto, ON M5RE 3E9 (416)538-8316, Fax (416)538-8027. LeahE@idirect.com.

Day Number 17

Today you'll concentrate on **selling your books to corporations**.

Sell Your Books to Corporations

Beyond the traditional markets of bookstores and libraries there is the wide world of quantity sales. Here's how to get going on quantity sales to corporate America:

- Start today by writing a letter to corporate offices across America that might be interested in your book. Think outside the box a little here: If you've got a book on organizing, maybe they'll be interested because you can teach their executives or sales force how to get more work accomplished; if your book is on life on the road or restaurants across America, maybe corporations will buy it to pass out to their traveling sales force. I billed my book, *Terrorism and Kids: Comforting Your Child* as an antidote to employee lateness and absenteeism for corporations whose employees were up all night with their children's nightmares.

- To find corporations and CEOs you can do the research yourself (see www.hoovers.com or www.forbes.com) or see the order form at the back of this book for information on our special report, *Sell Your Books to Corporations*, which includes a list of contact information for the top Fortune 100 companies.

- Don't forget to approach the CEOs and industry principals from whom you requested blurbs a few weeks ago: If they gave you a glowing quotation or review of the book, it should be easy to convince them or their underlings to buy several thousand copies for their employees.

- Each package should include a personalized letter explaining why the corporation should buy your book; promotional materials proving that it's a quality product; and a copy of your book. Tip: I send all my books numbered and signed—and bill them as first edition collector's items. This simple technique gets them past the secretary/screener's desk.

- Send the packages USPS Priority Mail, or courier them via FedEx or UPS to make an impact.

Day Number 18

Today you'll sign up with a **journalist referral service** or as an **online expert**.

Sign Up for Journalist Referrals

Most people try to capture the attention of media by initiating contact. But you'll be a lot more successful if you simply *respond* to media interest. Here's how:

- Sign up with a journalist referral service: They'll tell you which journalists are looking for info; you respond to anything relevant to your book. The more you respond, the more you'll be quoted, and the more books you'll ultimately sell. It's easy to do via email. Here are two possibilities:

  o PR Leads emails you targeted leads after finding out what topics you're interested in; the cost is $495 for one year and well worth the price. Contact Dan Janal at (952)380-1554, www.PRLeads.com, Dan@PRLeads.com.

  o SourceNet emails you *un*targeted leads, so you need to plow through the queries yourself. $95 per month. Or look through their list of requests, and just pay $35 for each journalist query to which you'd like to respond. www.Sourcenet.MediaMap.com.

- Sign up as an expert. There are several outfits that offer this service. ProfNet (www.ProfNet.com) is quite expensive, though among the best. (ASJA members can receive a free listing as part of their ASJA membership.)

- Finally, consider signing up for one or more newsletters that inform you of media needs:

  o *Book Marketing Update* by John Kremer is one of the best. Twice-monthly for $227 per year. Contact John at (800)796-6130, www.JohnKremer.com orders@bookmarket.com.

  o *Party Line* includes information on industry personnel changes. Weekly for $200/year. Contact Betty Yarmon at Party Line, 35 Sutton Place, New York, NY 10022, (212)755-3487, fax (212)755-4859, info@PartyLinePublishing.com.

  o InfoCom's *Bulldog Reporter* is an excellent, but expensive, source of media needs. Choose from several regional editions. Twice-monthly for $349. 5900 Hollis Street #R2, Emeryville, CA 94608, (800)959-1059, fax (510)596-9331, www.infocomgroup.com.

  o Joan Stewart's *Publicity Hound* is the bargain at $49.95 per year for issues every other week. Joan Stewart, 3930 Highway O, Saukville, WI 53080, (262)284-7451, fax (262)284-1737, wwwPublicityHound.com, JStewart@publicityhound.com.

Day Number 19

Today you'll **offer review copies to Amazon reviewers** and **join a professional association.**

Send Books to Top Amazon Reviewers

Amazon's top "laymen" reviewers post dozens of reviews each day. These reviews—particularly those of the top 100 reviewers—carry a lot of weight. Today, see if you can get some of these reviewers interested in your book. Here's how:

- Go online onto the Amazon site and sift through the list of top reviewers. You can look these reviewers up yourself, though Amazon doesn't make it easy to ferret out the information: Some listings include the reviewer's email address (make a note of it, and of what type of books they seem to prefer); others include hints about the reviewer (perhaps their hometown; check an online phonebook). Or you can check out our special report on contact information for Amazon's top 100 reviewers; see the order form at the back of this book.

- Email all the reviewers for whom you've been able to find addresses. Send individual emails— rather than a form letter—and explain a little about what your book is about, and why they might like to review it. Ask if they'd be interested in seeing it, and tell them you'd be happy to send them a complimentary copy.

- Each time you get back a positive response, send them a confirmation email, thanking them for their time, and pop a book in the mail to them; send the books USPS Priority Mail, or FedEx or UPS overnight. You might want to include some of your publicity materials and a personal note as well.

- Finally, be sure to email and thank every reviewer who does post a positive review. You can also ask if they'd mind if you included their comments on *your* website and publicity materials.

Join a Professional Association

Today, you'll also join a **professional association**. Here are some to consider:

- If you're an author but not a publisher, consider:

  o The American Society of Journalists Association (ASJA), 1501 Broadway #302, New York, NY 10036, (212)997-0947, ExecDir@ASJA.org, www.ASJA.org. $195 plus $100 initiation fee.

  o The Authors Guild, 31 East 28th Street, 10th floor, New York, NY 10016, (212)563-5904, fax (212)564-5363, staff@authorsguild.org, www.authorsguild.org. $90 per year.

- o The National Writers Union (NWU), 113 University Place, 6th floor, New York, NY 10003, (212)254-0279, nwu@nwu.org, www.nwu.org. $95-$155 depending on income.

- If you've published independently, definitely join the Publishers Marketing Association (PMA). PMA offers a high quality newsletter and range of low-cost educational programs and marketing opportunities. Jan Nathan, Publishers Marketing Association, 627 Aviation Way, Manhattan Beach, CA 90266, (310)372-2732, fax (310)374-3342, PMAOnline@aol.com, www.pma-online.org. $99.

- Both authors and publishers should also join Publishers Advocate, PO Box 590239, Newton, MA 02459-0002, info@PublishersAdvocate.com, www.PublishersAdvocate.com. Publishers Advocate distributes an online newsletter targeted at hundreds of booksellers and libraries, through which it announces members' books and talks as well as advocating for independent publishers. It also offers financial benefits to authors and publishers, including 5-20% off printing prices. $50.

- The Association of American Publishers is the oldest U.S. trade association for book publishers. It is expensive to join, and has only recently begun offering programs for smaller independent publishers.   Patricia Schroeder, Association of American Publishers, 71 Fifth Avenue, New York, NY   10003, (212)255-0200, fax (212)255-7007, www.publishers.org. $195.

- SPAN (Small Publishers of North America) also offers a worthwhile newsletter and display opportunities.   Marilyn Ross, SPAN, PO Box 1306, Buena Vista, CO   8211, (719)395-4790, fax (719)395-8374,   Span@Spannet.org, www.Spannet.org. $95.

Day Number 20

Today you'll pursue **catalog sales** and catch up on **loose ends**.

Pursue Catalog Sales

Catalogs buy non-returnable, pay shipping, and buy in large quantities—though they may want 80% discounts. Here's how to get started in selling to catalogs:

- To find out appropriate catalogs which might be interested in your book, check out the following largest catalog directories at your local library; some of them are also searchable online:

  o The Catalog Shop,
    www.thecatalogshop.com

  o Shop at Home Catalog,
    www.ShopAtHome.com

  o Buyer's Index (www.buyersindex.com)

  o Catalog City (www.catalogcity.com)

  o Catalog Link (www.CatalogLink.com)

  o The Directory of Business to Business Catalogs

  o Catalog of Catalogs

  o Catalog Central (www.catalogcentral.com)

    o Catalogs from A-Z (`www.catalogsfroma-z.com`)

- Once you have list of possibilities, call their toll-free number and request a catalog. Ask for the name of the book buyer, and their email address if possible. Request a submission form, if they have one.

- In addition to returning the submission form, send them a bulleted list of why your book would work well in their catalog. If you can write catalog copy in the style of their catalog, write a blurb describing your product so that they can envision it fitting into the catalog.

Tie Up Loose Ends

- By now you should have a selection of blurbs from celebrities and politicians. Follow up with a personal, handwritten thank you note to each— and enclose a signed copy of your book, if you didn't send one initially. While you're at it, enclose a few postcards; you never know where these might end up.

- If bookstores have been unable to procure your book because of distribution problems, do another email to the independent bookstores and note that, because you have been told bookstores are unsuccessfully trying to get it from Ingram or whomever, you will be happy to offer books directly until their inventory is up again. Offer the same terms Ingram gives them. Follow through promptly and politely. Be a pleasure to work with.

- Offer the BookSense stores an author tour or book signing.

- Congratulations if by now you've made it into the BookSense program! Don't forget to request BookSense stickers to put on your books showing that you've received this accolade. If you've published independently, consider going back for a quick redesign on your cover to incorporate the BookSense award sticker as a permanent part of the cover design. Whenever you send packages out—to the media, to the book clubs, to anyone important—put one of your BookSense stickers on the outside of your Priority Mail envelope. This draws people's attention—and gets your mail opened first.

- Don't forget to put your BookSense selection prominently on your website.

- Of course, once you make it onto the BookSense recommended list, follow up with everyone again. Send a thank you to the BookSense administrators, and send a heartfelt thank you (email is fine) to each of the stores.

- Send out press releases announcing to everyone that you've made the BookSense list.

- Re-do your postcard to include the BookSense selection—or sticker them yourself—and do a mailing to independent bookstores nationwide. See the order form at the back of this book for our Special Report on contacting independent bookstores; or participate in a cooperative mailing:

  o PMA, 627 Aviation Way, Manhattan Beach, CA 90266, (310)372-2732, fax (310)374-3342, www.Pma-Online.org

  o Sam Decalo, Florida Academic Press, PO Box 540, Gainesville, FL 32602. (352)332-5104, FAPress@worldnet.att.net

- Immediately offer to do something (a keynote speech at the ABA breakfast or lunch, speak at an educational session, help facilitate someone else's talk) at Book Expo America. Most BookSense authors don't know about BEA or care, so you have an advantage, and if you move fast, you'll get the slot just by persistence. When my book, *Terrorism and Kids: Comforting Your Child* won a BookSense selection, I immediately contacted Carl Lennertz and volunteered to do something at BEA. If you're the author, tell your publisher that you're interested in this—and then send the letter yourself, to make sure it happens.

- Stay in touch with your independent bookstores, particularly the ones who have responded with personal messages. Don't bug them—they get a lot of mail—but keep them informed of particularly great reviews, author tours and appearances, etc. These are invaluable contacts for you, and no one else is paying attention to them.

- Every so often—the frequency depends on the type of book—do a mailing to the independent bookstores again to keep them reordering. I've found postcard mailings to be particularly useful: They are not perceived as junk mail, they don't need to be opened, they can be easily stuffed into a to-do folder for later (and carry a visual reminder), they're not bulky like a press kit or brochure, and *other people get to see them* on the way to their destination.

- Fax the chains each time your book achieves any notoriety—a higher rating on Amazon, a blurb, an advance sale, etc.

- Email Library Journal to see if your book is scheduled for review. Include the title, author, publisher, publication date, and the date you sent the galley. LJQuery@Cahners.com, (212)463-6818.

- Remember to email or fax your contact list and update your progress chart.

This week you:

- Created a holiday

- Started working on quantity sales to organizations and corporations

- Signed up with a journalist referral service or as an online expert

- Sent review copies to top Amazon reviewers

- Joined a professional association

- Began book sales to catalogs

- Remembered to email or fax your contact list and update your progress chart

Congratulations! Your book is selling!

Week Number Five

CR BO

This week you'll:

- Get involved online
- Get involved with the independent bookstore publications and associations
- Organize your speaking tour
- Submit your book to home shopping shows
- Get a buzz going
- Email or fax your contacts list and update your progress chart

Day Number 21

Today you'll **get involved online** and make the most of your **professional associations.**

Get Involved Online

- A few days ago, you joined a professional association. Today, make the most of it. Send an announcement of your new title including the ISBN, retail price, number of pages, and any short review information. Make sure you include a web address or phone number so people can order it.

- While you're at it, join one or more of the free online communities in which independent publishers are active. Choose between a variety of moderated (less rancorous but somewhat less interesting) and moderated. The best known—and most interesting—is the pub-forum list. Send email to majordomo@majordomo.alentus.com with the word *subscribe pub-forum you@youremail.com* in the *body* (not the subject line) of the message.

- You may also want to consider the following publishing lists and communities:

  o SPAN's self-publishing list. Send email to Self-Publishing-Subscribe@yahoogroups.com.

- o Alt.Publish. Go to www.groups.google.com and search for alt.publish books.

- o About.Publishing. Go to www.Publishing.About.com.

- o BookZonePro—Go to www.BookZonePro.com.

- Both authors and publishers should make sure to join Publishers Advocate to keep up with the latest news in the book industry. See the Publishers Advocate appendix or sign up at www.PublishersAdvocate.com or by sending email to newsletter@PublishersAdvocate.com.

- You should also sign up for a few of the many online newsletters that will keep you informed about the book world in general. These are some of the best:

- o Foreword This Week. Sign up at www.ForewordMagazine.com/newsletter /newsletter.asp.

- o PW Daily. Sign up at www.PublishersWeekly.com (Scroll down on the left side toolbar.)

- o PW Newsline. Sign up at www.PublishersWeekly.com (Scroll down on the left side toolbar.)

    o   Publishers   Lunch.   Send   email   to `PublishersLunch-subscribe@Topica.com`.

- If you're not already, get involved online on a subject related to your book. Join a chat room or a list or a bulletin board discussion. Here's what to do:

  o Don't actively promote your book—that's not web etiquette—but offer useful hints and tips, and try to make the sorts of comments you'd make if you were in a professional situation and wanted to impress people unobtrusively.

  o Be sure to check for spelling and grammatical mistakes in your email—there's nothing that makes you look unprofessional faster than an error-ridden post.

  o Never use all capital letters in your posts—it's the online equivalent of SHOUTING.

  o Remember to always add a "signature" line or two below your name—this is where you can advertise your book. Don't forget to include your email address and website.

  o If you're having trouble keeping track of which lists you've joined and how to post to them, see `www.ListTool.com`.

Day Number 22

Today you'll become involved with the **independent bookstore associations and publications**.

Work With Independent Bookstores

One worthwhile publicity avenue that most authors and publishers miss is the world of independent bookstores. Here's how to get involved:

- First, join your local regional independent bookstore association. These organizations are in all parts of the country, and are much easier to "work" than the national organization, if only because they're more manageable in size. For a small membership fee you can join the association, attend its trade show, and read its newsletters. After a while, you'll get to know the players—and they'll get to know you. A full updated listing is available at www.bookweb.org.

- Attend the regional book show. If you go back year after year, you'll make friends and become a "known quantity" whom they'll recognize. Even if you only go once, you'll make an impact if you're friendly and outgoing. You can go for the expense of renting an exhibitor's booth, or you can just pass out your postcard to everyone you meet—and make sure you meet everyone! I always bring along some trinket or doodad to hand out at these shows, and the cleverer the better. Everyone and his brother is handing out key rings, pencils, and mugs; so I hand out more unusual items. When I was publicizing *The Infertility Diet*, for example, I passed out fortune cookies that said: "Wise man buy Infertility Diet and make fortune and many baby. Your lucky number is (617)630-0945 (my order number)." Booksellers gobbled them up.

- If you can't attend the regional shows yourself, be certain to send your book. Several organizations offer this service:

  o PMA, 627 Aviation Way, Manhattan Beach, CA 90266, (310)372-2732, fax (310)374-3342, PMAOnline@aol.com, www.pma-online.org

  o SPAN, PO Box 1306, Buena Vista, CO 8211, (719)395-4790, fax (719)395-8374, Span@Spannet.org, www.Spannet.org

  o Combined Book Exhibits, 277 White Street, Buchanan, NY 10511, (800)462-7687, fax (914)739-7575, info@CombinedBook.com, www.combinedbook.com. CBE offers face-out display opportunities at library shows for as low as $20 per title, once you've joined the program for $75.

  o Association Book Exhibits, 8727A Cooper Road, Alexandria, VA 22309, (703)619-5030, fax (703)619-5035, www.BookExhibit.com. ABE offers face-out display opportunities at library and special interest shows (such as psychological conventions) for $40-50 per title, lower if you join their program or exhibit many books.

- Consider joining the American Booksellers Association (ABA), 828 South Broadway, Tarrytown, NY 10591, (800)637-0037, fax (914)591-2720, Info@bookweb.org, www.Bookweb.org. The ABA is the national association of independent booksellers. The fee is now a steep $350 plus a $25 initiation fee.

- Whether or not you join the ABA, subscribe to their free weekly, now online, newsletter, *Bookselling This Week*, which will keep you up to date on all the national news concerning independent bookstores. You can sign up at the ABA site, www.BookWeb.org.

- If you have something interesting to say—about your book, about the publishing process, about your experiences as an author, about your reception by the independent bookstores or the rest of the publishing world—write a short editorial and send it for consideration to *Bookselling this Week*, 828 South Broadway, Tarrytown, NY 10591.

- If the national newsletter isn't interested, try sending it to your local, or any of the other regional independent organizations instead. Each of these organizations publishes a newsletter (some of them are monthlies, a few are less frequent). Be sure to include a thank you to the independent bookstores, naming names if there are any folks in particular who were helpful. And don't forget to include the info on your book at the end.

- Read Pat Holt's gritty *Holt Uncensored* online newsletter, for an appreciation of both the plight and pluckiness of independent booksellers. Subscribe by sending email to Pat@HoltUncensored.com.

- Subscribe to Publishers Advocate and help present the perspective of authors and independent publishers—including your new book and any related talks—to our natural allies, the independent bookseller world. Subscribe online at www.PublishersAdvocate.com or send email to newsletter@PublishersAdvocate.com.

Day Number 23

Today you'll plan your **speaking tour**.

Plan a Speaking Tour

Every author and publisher in search of a bestseller needs to consider a speaking tour. You won't *do* the speaking tour within the 30 days—but you need to plan it out far in advance. The reason is that many of the places you'll be speaking publish newsletters or catalogs publicizing their talks, and the deadlines for these publications are several months in advance of the talks. You need to plan where you're traveling as far in advance as possible, both so that you can maximize your speaking and so that you can minimize your travel expenses. Here's how to plan a dynamite speaking tour:

- First, break your speaking tour down by region. When a big New York City publishing house sends you on a cross-country publicity tour, they book it as one continuous trip, but that is not the most effective way for you to do it: You can get a better buzz going for your book by doing several smaller trips. Depending on how much travel you can afford, try to do at least a California trip (Californians buy the most books in the country) and a New York City trip; if you can afford to do more you might consider Chicago, D.C., Seattle, or other cities, depending on the nature of your book (a book on seniors, for example, should include a trip to Florida and other areas where retirement communities are concentrated.)

- Next, plan your travel to coincide with some regional event. You can do book publicity, including media interviews and speaking at bookstores, anywhere; try to work at least one professional or niche conference into each stop along your route to maximize the buzz for your buck. One possibility is to key your travel to the regional book shows, most of which take place in early fall. (Book Expo America is the big, national book show—which rotates between Los Angeles, Chicago, and New York—but unless you have time and money to spare, stick to the local regional book shows.) If you've gotten some attention from BookSense, see if you can arrange to speak at one or more of these shows. The shows only have a certain amount of space for authors to do the keynote speeches, but there are many other slots to fill, and you should definitely volunteer to fill them. Offer to autograph books (thereby getting your book into the hands of hundreds of booksellers personally.) If nothing else, offer to help staff the registration booth or take tickets at the dinner—thereby putting your name (and postcards!) squarely in front of everyone.

- Next, with each city, figure out your most desired speaking venues. Be sure to think about both general publicity (speaking at adult education forums, bookstores, and libraries) and targeted publicity (speaking at diet and fitness centers if your book is about weight loss; at hospital support groups if your book is about surviving cancer, and so forth.) Arrange to speak at:

o Adult Education Centers. Consider this: A small ad in the New York or Los Angeles Times costs several thousand dollars. But if you arrange to give a talk at the New York or Los Angeles Learning Annex, they'll run a full description of your book, including a photo and website, in their catalog—which is seen by a similarly sized and composed audience— for *free*. Not only that, but people are much more likely to pay attention to the information, because it's perceived as editorial, rather than advertising. Adult education places don't pay big bucks, but they're an invaluable source of publicity. And they'll let you sell your books and other products. In one evening in Los Angeles, I spoke to over 50 people, and sold enough books to cover the air and hotel expenses for the entire 2-week, 5-city tour. (Of course, neither turn-out—nor sales—are guaranteed.) You can announce your availability to dozens of adult education centers nationwide via an announcement in Publishers Advocate (see the appendix or www.PublishersAdvocate.com for more information). Or you can contact the individual centers directly. Here are some of the adult education centers that need speakers:

- Glendale Community College, Phoenix, AZ, (623)845-3333

- Paradise Valley Community College, Phoenix, AZ, (602)787-6802

- Butte County College, Oroville, CA

- California State University, Chico, CA, (530)898-6105

- Fresno Community College, Fresno, CA, (559)457-6015

- Los Angeles Learning Annex, 11850 Wilshire Blvd. #100, Los Angeles, CA 90025, (310)478-6677, fax (310)478-4854

- Modesto Community College, Modesto, CA, (209)575-6063

- Napa Valley College, Napa Valley, CA, (707)253-3070

- The Learning Exchange, 650 Howe Avenue #600, Sacramento, CA 95825, (916)929-9200, fax (916)929-0806, LeExchange@aol.com, www.sacweb.com/Learning

- San Diego Learning Annex, 520 West Ash #110, San Diego, CA 92101, (619)544-9700, fax (619)544-9734

- San Francisco Learning Annex, 291 Geary Street #510, San Francisco, CA 94102, (415)788-5500, fax (415)788-5574

- Arapahoe Community College, Community Education, 2500 West College Drive, PO Box 9002, Littleton, CO 80160, (303)797-5723, fax (303)797-5935

- Colorado Free University, 1510 York, Denver, CO 80206, (303)399-0093, fax (303)399-0477

- First Class, 1726 20th Street NW, Washington, DC 20009, (202)797-5102, fax (202)797-5104, FiClassInc@aol.com

- The Knowledge Shop, 1241 Semoran Blvd # 147, Casselberry, FL 32707, (407)671-9505

- The Knowledge Shop, Atlanta, GA, (678)766-6666

- The Discovery Center, 2940 N. Lincoln Avenue, Chicago, IL 60657, (773)348-8120, fax (773)880-6164

- Heartland Community College, 1226 Towanda Avenue, Bloomington, IL 61701, (309)827-0500, fax (309)827-8505, www.hcc.cc.il.us

- Ankeny School District, Des Moines, IA, (515)965-9606

- Cambridge Center for Adult Education, 42 Brattle Street, Cambridge, MA 02138, (617)547-6789, fax (617)497-7532, www.ccae.org

- Boston Center for Adult Education, 5 Commonwealth Avenue, Boston, MA 02116, (617)267-2465, fax (617)247-3606, www.Bcae.org

- Brookline Adult and Community Education, PO Box 150, Brookline, MA 02146, (617)730-2700, fax (617)730-2674, www.Brookline.mec.edu

- Learning for All Seasons, PO Box 579, Lexington, MA 02173, (781)861-0379, www.BostonBBS.org

- Newton Community Education, Newton North, 360 Lowell Avenue, Newtonville, MA 02160, (617)552-7461, fax (617)965-7654

- Pine Manor College, Adult Continuing Studies, 400 Heath Street, Chestnut Hill, MA 02167, (617)731-7176

- Winchester Recreation and Community Education, 15 High

Street, Winchester, MA 01890, (617)721-7125, fax (617)721-7129, Mary_Johnson@Winchester.Mec.Edu

- Delta College, Delta & Mackinaw Roads, University Center, MI 48710, (517)686-9413, fax (517)686-8736, www.Delta.edu

- Waverly Community Schools, 3131 W. Michigan Avenue, Lansing, MI 48917, (517)484-5600, fax (517)484-3817

- Harding Community Education, St. Paul, MN, (651)293-8733

- Central Missouri University, Office of Extended Campus, Humphreys 403, Warrensburg, MO 64093, (816)543-4615, fax (816)543-8333, www.cmsul.cmsu.edu

- Communiversity, UMKC, 5327 Holmes, Kansas City, MO 64110, (816)235-1448, fax (816)235-5612, www.cctr.umkc.edu

- University of Missouri, Kansas City, MO, (816)235-1448, 5277

- University of Nevada, Las Vegas, NV, (702)895-3011

- The New York Learning Annex, 16 East 53rd Street, 4th floor, New York, NY 10022, (212)371-0280, fax (212)319-1623

- The Seminar Center, 1776 Broadway #1001, New York, NY 10019, (212)655-0077, fax (212)655-0088

- Duke University, Continuing Education, PO Box 90707, Durham, NC 27708, (919)684-3255, fax (919)681-8235, www.Learnmore.Duke.edu

- Mt. Airy Learning Tree, 7101 Germantown Avenue, Philadelphia, PA 19119, (215)247-5511, fax (215)248-1903

- Temple University, Office of Special Programs, 580 Meetinghouse Road, Ambler, PA 19002, (215)283-1308, fax (215)283-1419, www.vm.temple.edu

- Learning Connections Inc., 201 Wayland Avenue, Providence, RI 02906, (401)274-9330, fax (401)521-3910, www.BDol.com

- University of Tennessee Community Programs, 600 Henley Street #105, Knoxville, TN 37996, (423)974-0150, fax (423)974-0264, www.gateway.cc.utk.edu

- Fun/Ed, 13608 Midway Road, Dallas, TX 75244, (972)960-2666, fax (972)960-6355

- Leisure Learning Unlimited, PO Box 22675, Houston, TX 77227, (713)529-4414, fax (713)877-1890, www.llu.com

- University of Texas, Austin, TX, (512)232-5277

- University of Utah, Continuing Education, 2167 Annex Building, Salt Lake City, UT 84112, (801)585-3093, www.admin.dce.utah.edu

- Discovery University, Rte 5, Box 448, Lexington, VA 24450, (703)463-2248

- Discover University, 2601 Elliott Avenue #4305, Seattle, WA 98121, (206)443-0447, fax (206)443-0912, www.eskimo.com/~discover

- Lower Columbia College, Longview, WA, (360)575-6695

- Tacoma Community College, Gig Harbor, WA, (253)566-6031

- Tacoma Community College, Tacoma, WA, (253)566-6031

o Libraries: Libraries are always looking for authors and speakers—and unlike adult education centers and bookstores, they will *pay* for talks if you have an interesting or topical book. You can write directly to libraries in the cities to which you'll be traveling, or you can post an announcement of your (fee or free) talk on Publishers Advocate, which is emailed to hundreds of librarians, booksellers, and adult education center directors weekly. See the appendix or www.PublishersAdvocate.com for more information.

o Bookstores: Independent and chain bookstores are always eager for talks and signings.

- To arrange programs through Barnes & Noble Author Promotions, contact Jennifer Gardener at (212)633-4082 and ask her to send the 30-page list of stores and contacts nationwide.

- To arrange programs at Borders, contact the individual stores' community relations coordinator (programmer).

- To arrange programs in the independent bookstores, put an announcement in Publishers Advocate, which is emailed to hundreds of booksellers weekly. See

> the appendix or
> www.PublishersAdvocate.com for
> more information.

 o You can also arrange to speak at synagogues and churches, civic groups, schools, parent associations, teacher meetings, clubs, corporations, book fairs, Rotary, Kiwanis, and Lions clubs, community centers, YMCAs, and more. Try a program or a signing at a grocery store, a laundromat, or anyplace else particularly relevant to your title.

- Consider this: Book signings are not always successful. But demonstrations and programs can be quite successful. Don't plan to just do a signing; make it an event. Do a cooking demonstration or a dramatic reading; teach kids to do origami or finger knit. Think outside the box when you're arranging events.

- Once you've booked your cornerstone talks, don't forget to announce your availability to the broadcast media along the way. Contact producers directly, or consider an ad in Radio-TV Interview Report, (800)553-8002, www.rtir.com, which is mailed to over 4,000 broadcast producers nationwide.

- Get a large, sturdy manila envelope for *each* city to which you'll be traveling, and put all your itineraries, tickets, directions, packing lists, and leads inside. On the outside of the envelope, make a list of the days and dates you'll be in the city, and under the appropriate date, the contact names, addresses, and phones for each of your speaking engagements. Put a small checkmark next to each contact once you have (inside the envelope!) all the information you need for that speech—confirmation letters, contracts, driving directions, number of books they're expecting you to bring—and have given *them* all the information they need—press announcements, how they should introduce you, your social security number, etc. The envelope will be a visual reminder of which arrangements are all set, and which are still in limbo. Don't forget to ask your contact at each speaking engagement to fax you a list of media contacts for their area. You'll use that list to announce your talk to the media—and to book television and radio shows en route.

- Before you go, consider testing out your talk at a Toastmasters meeting. Toastmasters is a great organization if you feel your speech still needs practice; you can find a local chapter (and attend, practicing your talk in front of a live supportive audience) at www.Toastmasters.org.

- Send an announcement of your talk to your mailing list of area customers, many of whom may want to hear your information again or meet you in person to ask more specific questions.

- Notify local booksellers and librarians of your talk, so they'll be sure to stock books in time to meet the demand you'll be generating. (See the order form at the back of this book for information on *The Independent Bookstore Publicity Kit*.)

- Send your itinerary to your wholesalers and distributors, so they'll be sure to have books in stock for local libraries and bookstores who will order to meet the demand. (You can make sure Ingram has enough stock by checking their stock status line at (800) 937-0995.)

- Send an announcement to the American Booksellers Association *Bookselling This Week* announcing your itinerary, so that bookstores will order copies in anticipation of your talk. Write to the American Booksellers Association, 828 South Broadway, Tarrytown, NY 10591, Info@Bookweb.org.

- Be sure to alert the local media in each town about your upcoming talk. A simple press release to the local calendar section is sure to be printed, and may generate interest in a feature.

- At your talks, be sure to remember the following:

  o Make sure everyone receives an order form, brochure, or postcard. Try to see if you can put a book on each chair in the room—after fondling the book for an hour while you speak, most people will want to own it.

     o Sell books directly at the program—if you don't have official credit card slips with you, you can have people write their charge card number on the back of their business cards.

     o If you run out of books at your talk, have people write down their contact information, and promise to get books to them within the week. Then call your order department or your spouse, and have them get those books into the mail immediately.

     o In bookstores, don't forget to sign the books before you go home—they're less likely to be returned if they're signed. (Affix an *autographed* sticker to the front cover of the book to increase the perceived value.)

- Remember to send a press release to the media *after* you give the talk—reporting again on the content of the talk (and incidentally your book) and citing the turnout, if it was high or unusual in any way. (If you prepare the fax numbers and press releases before you leave home, it's much easier to keep up with sending them out while on the road.)

- Follow-up the speech with a brief thank you letter or press release to the venue's newsletter. Library association newsletters, for example, will always print a follow-up feature for any successful program they've run. (Bring your camera to the talk so you can snap a photo of you and the organizer, and that will get into most newsletters as well. Be sure to hold up the book for the photo!)

- Every state library system has a newsletter—none of which runs reviews. Instead, write an essay about your library experiences in the state, or a press release of your recent library talk—and be sure to work in the title of your book (and ISBN) at the same time.

- Before you leave on your tour, check the Ingram and Baker & Taylor inventory status of your book. If there aren't enough books in the regions to which you're heading, be sure you notify your buyer of your speaking schedule so they'll replenish their warehouses. You can check Ingram stock status by calling (800) 937-0995.

- Make sure you've made arrangements to ship books to your destination cities well in advance. You can't possibly carry enough books on the plane—and you want to get your books mailed as early as possible, just in case they get lost en route and you need to send a replacement shipment.

- If you are comfortable speaking, and get good reviews from audiences, but feel poorly equipped to pursue speaking engagements on your own, consider a speakers bureau. The big speakers bureaus won't consider you until you've given at least a thousand speeches, but if you are a niche speaker (that is, if you are an expert on one particular topic) consider signing on with Andrea

Reynolds' *Experts Who Speak.* You can get more
information at www.ExpertsWhoSpeak.org.

Day Number 24

Today you'll submit your book to the **home shopping networks**.

Appear on Home Shopping Shows

Home Shopping Shows sell millions of different products—including books. If your book retails for between $15 and $30, and has some sort of demonstration capability, you might be able to sell to the home shopping networks. This won't work for some books, but for others, it can be a goldmine. Here's what you need to know:

- Books are purchased in large quantity at 50% discount, returnable, they pay shipping both directions.

- Contact the shows and ask for a vendor application.

  o QVC, 275 Main Street, Mount Kisco, NY 10549, (914)242-7190, fax (914)242-7196, www.qvc.com

  o Home Shopping Network New Business Development, 1 HSN Drive, St. Petersburg, FL 33729, (800)436-1010, fax (727)872-7292, vendorR@hsn.net, www.hsn.com

Day Number 25

Today you'll **start a buzz** going and catch up on **loose ends**.

Buzz Your Book

There has been a lot written recently about the concept of starting a "buzz" going about your book. Basically, "buzz" is when people start to talk, and tell their friends, and they start to talk, and on it goes, building and building, until you've got enough critical mass talking about your book that it has a momentum all its own. Here's how:

- You are the best person to buzz your book. You know the content the best, are the most passionate about its contents, and know the market better than anyone else. You have the enthusiasm to generate buzz—and the motivation to keep it going.

- Send email to friends and fans. Email is one of the easiest—and certainly the cheapest—ways to generate buzz. If you can compose humorous updates on your book, so much the better: Humor circulates particularly well on the internet.

- For a comprehensive understanding of buzz and what makes it work, I highly recommend Malcolm Gladwell's bestselling book, *The Tipping Point*, the book that was responsible for pioneering the concept of buzz and how some products or concepts skyrocket from obscurity to fame.

Tie Up Loose Ends

- Once the chain bookstores have accepted your book, send a thank you note quickly. You might want to send your contacts a signed copy of the book as well, to express your gratitude. It's gestures like this that make you stand out from the crowd.

- Send postcards to all your friends and acquaintances telling them about your new book. (Rather than asking them to buy a copy, you might feel more comfortable suggesting they ask for the book at their local library. Don't worry—this will fuel sales, too.)

- Today, follow up on catalog sales. Phone to make sure the catalogs have received your application. Ask if they'd like to see the actual book (if they say yes, send it along with the catalog copy and bulleted list again—just in case.) Continue to email or phone every two weeks until you get an answer. Be tenacious!

- By now you should have some news on book clubs. If you've sold to any book clubs, make sure you send out a press release, via email or fax, announcing your success. That's news!

- Don't keep your contact list in the dark—send your wholesalers, distributors, and bookstores all your news. Every week, at least at the beginning, send an updated promotional schedule, speeches you've booked, blurbs you've cornered, etc.

- It's time to compose a letter to include with all your outgoing individual orders. Thank your readers for purchasing your books. Encourage them to write a blurb, or a review for Amazon, Barnes and Noble, and Books-A-Million. Send them a postcard, and encourage them to post it in a café or ice cream parlor in their hometown or pass it along to their local librarian, bookstore, or newspaper. Notify them of upcoming talks or programs related to your subject, and encourage them to keep checking your website for updated information. Word of mouth is your best pr, and customers your most likely prospects for business. Make them feel wanted!

- Remember to email or fax your contacts, and update your progress chart.

This week you:

- Got involved online

- Got involved with the independent bookstore publications and associations

- Organized your speaking tour

- Submitted your book to home shopping shows

- Got a buzz started

- Emailed or faxed your contacts list and updated your progress chart

Congratulations! You're almost done!

Week Number Six

Cʒ ঽᴖ

This week you'll:

- Initiate foreign rights sales
- Initiate other sales
- Syndicate your writing
- Begin selling your special reports
- Start an email newsletter
- Start planning your next book!

Day Number 26

Today you'll begin pursuing **foreign rights sales** and **other sales.**

Make Foreign Sales

Foreign rights sales can mean some additional cash, or for some books, big bucks. Not all titles are appropriate for foreign sales, but if you have a title that might sell abroad—and certainly anything in the business or psychology arena—don't neglect the opportunity for international exposure and profits. Here's how to get started:

- Send your book overseas to one of the foreign rights fairs—the Frankfurt Book Fair is the largest of these, London Book Fair is second. The cheapest way to do this is via PMA or Foreword Magazine, both of which will display your book, face out, for a nominal fee. After the show, they will send you information on which foreign agents stopped by their booth, and which of these, if any, expressed interest in your book. You may even want to sign up with both services: The book shows are very large and crowded, and the more exposure your book gets, the more likely it is to be noticed. Sign up to be included:

    o Publishers Marketing Association, 627 Aviation Way, Manhattan Beach, CA 90266, (310)372-2732, fax (310)374-3342, PMAOnline@aol.com, www.pma-online.org

o   Foreword Magazine, 129½ East Front Street, Traverse City, MI 49684, (231)933-3699, fax (231)933-3899,
    www.ForewordMagazine.com

- If you didn't get interest from foreign agents at the show—don't give up! It's not unusual. The shows are big and overwhelming, and there are far too many books competing for attention. You're going to garner most of your interest *after* the show, by following up with the vendors who *weren't* interested in your book.

- Send all foreign agents a copy of your book along with your promotional materials. Mention that they may have seen it exhibited at the PMA or Foreword Magazine booth.

- Another route is to send letters to foreign agents from the list in Bowker's *International Literary Market Place*, which you can find at your local library.

- Once you have interest from a foreign agent, they will probably request that you send copies of the book to all the foreign agents in other countries with whom they have relationships. Don't miss this opportunity: Beyond sending the book itself, be sure to include a letter explaining why the book will be of interest to people in their country, and include any publicity materials which might be of interest.

- Finally, continue to follow up with your foreign agent in the upcoming months. Sooner or later, persistence will result in sales.

Try Other Sales

Depending on your title, there may be other obvious—and less obvious—places to sell your book. Here are some ideas to get you started:

- If you have a book appropriate for a museum gift shop, this can be a wonderful venue. Try The Museum Store Association, 4100 E. Mississippi Avenue #800, Denver, CO 80246, (303)504-9223, fax (303)504-9585, www.museumdistrict.com. Or, check out *The Official Museum Directory* at your local library.

- Write to the authors of similar or related books— particularly authors whose work you referenced in your book or bibliography—and see if they'd be interested in mentioning your book in *their* next edition.

- The Children's Educational Cooperative offers newsletters, advertising, and other ways to promote your educational books to teachers, parents, schools, daycares and camps. $49/year. See www.childrens-educational-coop.com for more information.

- Check out www.nps.gov if you have an appropriate title for the National Park Service, or www.zoos.com if you have a title appropriate for a zoo.

- Think about banks, trade associations, insurance companies, pharmaceutical companies. Think about selling your book in stores that aren't bookstores.

- Check out The Thomas Register of American Manufacturers for lists of companies that might be interested giving or selling your book to its members.

- For a religious or spiritual title, try The Church and Synagogue Library Association, PO Box 19357, Portland, OR 97280, (503)244-6919, csla@worldaccesnet.com, www.worldaccessnet.com/~csla.

- Try selling to colleges through the National Association of College Stores, 500 East Lorain Street, Oberlin, OH 44074, (800)622-7498, fax (440)775-4769, www.nacs.org, products@nacs.org.

- If you have a product that might interest teachers, try Books Are Fun (now owned by Reader's Digest), 1680 Highway I, Fairfield, IA 52556, (641)472-7402 or (800)864-4941, fax (641)472-7402, BAF_Submissions@BooksAreFun.com, www.BooksAreFun.com.

Day Number 27

Today you'll initiate the process of **syndicating your writing**.

Syndicate Yourself

One overlooked source of exposure (and ultimately book sales) is syndication. If you know enough about a topic to have written an entire book, you know enough to write a weekly newspaper column. (Just think about it—surely in your 200 or 300 page book there must be 50 pages of interesting material? That's a year of newspaper columns.) Here are some things to consider when considering syndicating:

- Aside from the obvious publicity benefits—a national weekly newspaper column with the same title as your book, and contact information on how to buy the book, really can't be beat—self-syndication is also a great source of income. Let's say you're able to sell your column to only 50 publications, at only $10 each (a pretty conservative and low-ball estimate for a column on almost any topic.) That's $500 per week—or over $25,000 per year—just for tooting your own horn, with material you've already written. It doesn't get a whole lot better than that.

- Syndication has a certain mystique associated with it, but in reality, like working with the media in general, it's easier to get a lot of columns into many smaller publications than one big article into a larger publication. So shoot for the smaller publications.

- There are many syndication services whose job it is to screen your writing, and if they like you, they will distribute you to newspapers. You can go this route, the same way you can find a literary agent or a distributor, and part with a share of the profits in return for letting them handle the scutwork. Or you can do the legwork yourself— and keep the income.

- If you're going to self-syndicate, announce the availability of your column through the bible for newspapers looking for syndicated columns, *Editor and Publisher* magazine. They also publish an annual directory of all the available national columns, from which newspapers can pick and choose. (At only $8.50 this directory is a low-cost way to get a look at what the competition is offering.)

  o Editor and Publisher, 770 Broadway, New York, NY 10003, (646)654-5270, fax (646)654-5370, `CSullivan@EditorAndPublisher.com`, `www.editorandpublisher.com`

- Start by putting together a packet of your ten best articles. (That's right—take them straight out of the book.) Make the articles a uniform size, one that you feel comfortable cutting your material down into. Then do a word count. Syndicated columns range in length, but it's easiest to sell a column of 600 to 800 words. Make up at least ten or 20 packets.

- Add a jazzy cover letter, explaining your credentials for writing the column, and why the newspapers' readers will be interested. You can either tell them your charge (start with $5-10 per article, at least until you become a known quantity) or sit back and wait to see what size checks arrive; there are proponents in both camps.

- As newspapers pick up your column, change the cover letter that you send to reflect this: "My column is carried by over 30 newspapers all across the country…"

- Don't forget to send *Editor and Publisher* a press release announcing the availability of your column—and send another when you hit first 50, then 100, newspapers. Send your news to managing editor J.J. McGrath at JMCGrath@editorandpublisher.com.

- At first the few checks you receive may not feel worth the effort, but don't look on this as a profit center: Look at it as free newspaper space, without having to pay for an ad. Once you get going, you may find that you're selling many more books through your columns—and that the newspaper pay, alone, is keeping the mortgage paid.

- If your book is related to internet marketing, promotion, advertising, business, or sales, be sure to syndicate yourself online for no charge at www.web-source.net. If selected, your 400-1200 word article could be displayed on as many as 2,000 websites and 10,000 email newsletters.

- If you'd like more information on how to get started on self-syndication, see the order form for information on the *Syndicate Yourself Kit*.

Day Number 28

Today you'll begin creating and selling **special reports**.

Produce Special Reports

Another way to maximize sales from your book is to sell a series of related special reports. If you have developed content that is tangential to the book itself, or that is too "valuable" to be included in the book, you have the makings of a special report. Here are some things to think about:

- You can sell this material in the form of another book or booklet (be sure to include the order information at the end of your book!) or as an electronic or email mailing off your website.

- For many authors, special reports are bringing in more money than the original book, and it's easy to see why: Having "captured" a mailing list that is interested in your topic, it's easier to sell related (and more expensive!) products.

- From your book or related research, sift out the highest quality material and package it up as a series of "special reports."

- Special reports can be any length, any price, and on any topic.

- Add promotional announcements of these special reports to all your publicity materials—your book (include this information on your last page order form), your website, your email signature, your postcards.

- Include information on *all* the products and special reports you sell in each of the special reports. (If you sell three special reports, they should each include purchasing information on each of the other reports.)

- Don't forget to mention your special reports in your syndicated columns and in your email newsletter (which we'll talk about next.)

- Finish packaging up your special reports, and begin selling them from your website.

- If you'd like more information on how to create, publish, and effectively market special reports, see the order form for the *Special Reports Kit.*

Day Number 29

Today you'll create an **email newsletter**.

Publish an Email Newsletter

A complementary publicity tool for your book is an email newsletter. This can be a great way to sell more books, particularly if you are developing other related products that you can sell in addition. Here's how to begin:

- If you're active on a number of related internet lists, targeting an email newsletter to that population is an easy way to add to your income and increase your book sales noticeably.

- Simply clip out a page of your book's content each week to mail out as a separate tip or installment.

- Include information on your email newsletter in your email signature, so that interested people will know where to sign up.

- Don't forget to include easy instructions on how to subscribe (and unsubscribe) at the bottom of each and every newsletter you send out. (People may forward their newsletter on to friends or other lists, and you want everyone who likes it to be able to sign up easily.)

- Send information on the new email newsletter to all the people who have signed up on your website, or who have purchased books or products from you in the past. This is your natural audience.

- See the order form at the back of this book for our *Email Newsletter Kit* on the fastest way to get an email newsletter up and running.

Day Number 30

Today you'll catch up on **loose ends** and begin to **plan your next book!**

Tie Up Loose Ends

- Follow up with the major reviewers, by sending everyone who received a galley a finished book. If they have reviewed the book, it's a wonderful courtesy (and may favorably dispose them towards your next book); if they haven't reviewed the book, this may prompt them. Don't forget to send thank you notes to those who did review it. Few people bother to do this—so the impact will be even greater.

- Now that they've been selling your book for a while, contact all the chains again and ask how it's going. If they've sold a lot of your books, ask whether they have plans to model it. (*Modeling* is when, rather than simply ordering a few books and letting them go out of stock in the stores, the buyer decides that yours will be a serious seller, and allocates a certain buy for some number of the stores nationally. Each time a book sells in one of the stores, the book is automatically reordered. Modeling can transform a good chain seller to a perennial chain seller! (If you have a related book coming out soon, let them know that, too.)

- Finalize the travel arrangements for your speaking tour. Don't forget to pre-address a stack of your postcards so that you can send out your thank you notes as you travel; it will be one fewer thing to do when you get home. Also, be sure you make careful notes in your travel binder about details you wish you had done differently, contacts you need to follow up on, and so forth.

- Keep track of the BookSense editorial schedule so that you know when to approach the bookstores again for inclusion in the BookSense special issues. The nomination schedule for 2002 was as follows, but contact Carl Lennertz (Carl@BookSense.com) for a current schedule:

January	Science Fiction/Fantasy BookSense "Top Ten"
	Art/Design/Photo "Top Ten"
February	Poetry "Top Ten"
March	Spring Children's
	Teen "Top Ten"
April	Audio books "Top Ten"
June	Mystery "Top Ten"
	Fall Children's
September	Holiday/Children's

Keep in mind that more categories—including African American, travel, nature, women's studies, gay/lesbian, cookbooks, home and garden, mind/body/spirit, sports, science, scholarly/technical, university press, religion, business/finance, and reading group favorites— are being considered and added, so stay on top of the latest announcements of categories (www.BookSense.com).

- Follow up with the corporate offices on quantity sales. Contact each of the corporations to which you mailed packets and ask whether you can supply more information, or if they have everything they need to make their decision. Keep track of the names of secretaries and assistants—these are invaluable contacts. As soon as you've made one sale—of any size—add that fact to your sales letter to the rest, and drop it into your follow-up phone calls: "I'm just putting together a quantity order for Nike, which just ordered 50,000 copies for their employees; I wondered whether IBM had reached a decision yet on this purchase?"

- If you're trying to syndicate your material, send out another batch of packets this week. Don't forget to update your letter to reflect the numbers of newspapers already using your column.

- Follow up with the home shopping shows today. Keep up the contact with these shows every few weeks until you get an answer. Sometimes all it takes is time.

- Email or phone your catalog possibilities, and make sure they've received your book. Ask whether they need more information of any sort—and tell them you'll call back in a few weeks to see if they're closer to a decision.

- Continue to email or phone your catalogs every two weeks until you get an answer. Be tenacious! Remember that most catalogs plan their content at least six months in advance.

- If you get a nibble from a catalog company that wants to try a small number to see how it draws, follow up immediately. (If you're the author, make sure your publisher follows up on this quickly.)

- Remember to email or fax your contact list (and keep doing this weekly or monthly for the life of all your books!) and update your progress chart.

- Check with Foreword Magazine to see if your book is scheduled for review: Email Reviews@ForewordMagazine.com.

- Remember to keep thinking outside the box. For example: Studies show that over 50% of Americans say they'd like to receive a book as a holiday gift. So if your book is coming out in December, why not affix a fancy gold "Happy Holidays" sticker to improve your book sales?

- Once you've got the momentum, keep the pressure up. Doing only three things a day amounts to over 1,000 publicity pushes per year. Even if you're working another job (and if you do this right you won't have to moonlight for long!) you should be able to do three things a day.

Plan For the Next Book

You're almost done! Now is the time to begin planning—for your *next* bestseller.

- When you go back for another printing of your book, be sure to include some of the reviews and quotations you've garnered on the back cover or in the front of the book. Remember to update the copyright page and change it to say "second printing." If you've generated any new special reports, be sure to add these to your back-of-the-book order form.

- Start thinking now about the next book you're going to do. And try, *try* to write another book about the *same* topic. Aside from the fact that you can probably write your next book much more quickly (because you already know the issues) and can market it more effectively (because you know where to find the audience, and have developed an in-house list of buyers interested in that topic), you will also *sell more books*—because any customer, confronted in a bookstore with several books, two of whom are written *by the same person* will, all things being equal, buy one of those books—because the author looks more authoritative, simply by virtue of the fact that she's written two books on the same topic.

- One more idea for you: Once you have several books out on the same topic, you will have propelled yourself to that elusive "expert" status—and people will write to *you*, asking you to write blurbs for their books. Do it—it's the easiest way to get your name and book title out there! (And if they don't write to ask you—write to them with your quotation, anyway!) Spend some time to write a catchy, pithy, quotable quotation—so that you will be the one selected for the back cover and publicity material!

- Finally, if you will have several titles in the same niche, you can market them together (with perhaps a discount for readers who order the whole set) and you won't have to re-create the wheel each time you set out to market your new book.

This week you:

- **Initiated foreign rights sales**
- **Syndicated your writing**
- **Began selling your special reports**
- **Started an email newsletter**
- **Remembered to email or fax your contact list and updated your project chart**
- **Started planning your next book!**

Congratulations! If you've followed this plan, your book should be selling like hotcakes!

This concludes the daily 30-day plan to make your book a bestseller. In the following appendices, you can read more details about some of the basic components you'll need for your book (or you can order the prequel to this book, *The Publishing Game: Publish a Book in 30 Days* to get the complete story on how to begin your career as a publisher.)

But you already know enough to get started—so if you've just been reading, but not following, the steps in this plan, now it's time to put down this book and *start selling your own!* I wish you the best of luck. Please write and let me know how it goes. Send me your thoughts, ideas, comments, corrections (and anything you wish I'd included but didn't) to: BestsellerComments@PublishingGame.com.

Appendix A: Bibliography

Before you go home, there are a few other books and resources you should know about. There are a quazillion books on the market about self publishing and self-promotion, and I'm only recommending here the ones I personally found particularly useful. There are many others, and many that are not yet on the market. Read as many as you can get your hands on. Even a book that offers one interesting tip or one new idea is worth the time you've spent on it. All it takes is one brilliant new idea to make a bestseller.

Dan Poynter's books are the bibles of the self-publishing industry. Be sure to get the latest copy of his *The Self-Publishing Manual*. No one should be independently publishing without reading this book first.

Equally essential is John Kremer's *1001 Ways to Market Your Book*. This book is jam packed full of marketing ideas—too many to assimilate in a month, much less a sitting. But you'll find yourself coming back to this book again and again.

If you like the day-by-day organization of this book, try my prequel, *The Publishing Game: Publish a Book in 30 Days*, for a complete 30-day plan that explains how to go from manuscript to printed book.

On the other hand, if you've decided after reading this that publishing is way too much work, and you'd rather just write your books and let someone else sell them, try reading *The*

Publishing Game: Find an Agent in 30 Days. (Just so you know—I did—three times.)

Marilyn and Tom Ross's *The Complete Guide to Self-Publishing* contains much valuable information and is also considered one of the classics in the field.

Pat Bell's *THE PrePublishing Handbook: What You Should Know BEFORE You Publish Your First Book* provides a valuable overview of the pre-publishing process that will be immensely helpful to new publishers.

Shel Horowitz's *Grassroots Marketing: Getting Noticed in a Noisy World* is a wonderful tome on all aspects of garnering publicity.

Guerrilla Marketing for Writers by Jay Conrad Levinson, Rick Frishman, and Michael Larsen is also well worth a read.

If you're looking for a comprehensive book on various facets of publishing, check out Judith Appelbaum's *How to Get Happily Published.*

Appendix B: ISBN Numbers and Bar Codes

If you are going to sell your book in bookstores and libraries, you must have an ISBN. ISBN stands for International Standard Book Number. This worldwide identification system for books ensures that books are identified, ordered, and shipped correctly. Each edition of a book requires a unique ISBN. The ISBN appears on both the back cover of the book and on the copyright page. R. R. Bowker is the U.S. registry of ISBNs, and the only place to get an ISBN.

You can't order just one ISBN from Bowker: They charge $225 for ten ISBNs, and a whopping $800 for 100 ISBNs. The bad news is that everyone in the publishing industry can tell by your ISBN if you've purchased a block of ten or 100, so if you want to present yourself as a serious independent publisher, as opposed to a one-book self-published author, you'll need to go for the larger, more expensive block.

Bowker's turn-around time for ISBNs is ten business days from receipt of the completed form. After Bowker processes your payment, they'll send you a list of your ISBNs, and you'll select which ISBN you'd like to use for each book you publish.

Ask for the application form from: R. R. Bowker, 630 Central Avenue, New Providence, NJ   07974, (908)771-7755, fax (908)665-2895,   isbn-san@bowker.com, www.isbn.org/standards/home/isbn/us/printable/isbn.asp.

Once you have your ISBN, you can get a barcode for your book. The barcode—much like a supermarket barcode—can be scanned to identify the title, author, publisher, edition (hard or softcover), and price. All wholesalers and bookstores require books they carry to have such a barcode.

The barcode specific to books is called the "Bookland EAN/13 with add on" and it is printed on the back cover of your book, right below the ISBN number. You can buy a barcode yourself (they'll send you the film for the back cover directly; you'll need to supply the size desired and ISBN number) or, preferably, let your cover artist take care of this arrangement. The barcode costs between $10 and $40 and is available from a variety of vendors: Bowker can send you an updated list of suppliers upon request.

Appendix C: ABI Form

Another form you should fill out is the ABI, which stands for Advance Book Information form. By filling out the ABI form your book will be listed in the Bowker directory, *Books in Print*. You can do this at www.Bowkerlink.com or by writing R. R. Bowker, 630 Central Avenue, New Providence, NJ 07974, (908)771-7755, fax (908)665-2895, for an ABI guidebook and form. There is no charge for this listing. Remember to fill out two forms (with different ISBNs) if you are planning on both a hardcover and softcover edition.

One of the pieces of information you'll need for the ABI form is your official publication date. Bear in mind that what they're asking for is *not* the date you get books from the printer. What they want to know is your *official* publication date. Set this at least three to six months out. You'll want to do all the steps in this book before your official publication date—and then give yourself a few extra months just in case.

Appendix D: Library Numbers and Cataloging

The Library of Congress in Washington oversees several programs designed to facilitate the way libraries nationwide acquire and catalog books. The first two—the PCN and CIP programs—are programs by which the Library of Congress assigns a unique identification number to the catalog record for each book in its catalogued collections. (This information is printed on the copyright page of the book.) The programs are mutually exclusive, and you'll only need one of these: Once a book has a PCN it is ineligible for CIP data.

PCN stands for Preassigned Card Number. CIP stands for Cataloging in Publication. Both facilitate cataloging. The main difference between the two is that the catalog record of books with CIP data is distributed to libraries, book dealers, and bibliographic networks worldwide (via the Library of Congress' Machine Readable Cataloging [MARC] Distribution Service) to facilitate orders and cataloging. Cataloging information for books with just a PCN are *available*—but are not distributed. A second difference is that the CIP data includes the desired Dewey and LC classification numbers; the PCN does not.

All books acquired by libraries will need either the PCN or the CIP data. Libraries prefer CIP data—and are more likely to purchase books that contain the CIP than the PCN— because the cataloging records are already prepared. Furthermore, certain libraries buy books in certain CIP categories *sight unseen* each year. Even Baker & Taylor gets their notification of new titles via the Library of Congress' CIP records. Obviously, it is in your best interests to acquire the CIP data, rather than the PCN.

The Library of Congress, however, is reluctant to open the CIP program to small independent publishers (and offers the PCN as a second-rate substitute). The eligibility for the CIP program states: "Only U.S. publishers who publish titles that are likely to be widely acquired by U.S. libraries are eligible to participate in the CIP program. Self-publishers (i.e. authors and editors who pay for or subsidize publication of their own works) and publishers who mainly publish the works of only one or two authors are ineligible. Publishers ineligible for the CIP program may be eligible for the PCN Program."

There is (of course) a way around the Library of Congress's obstructions, and that is to present yourself as a big publishing house: Submit information on your next ten books, including ISBNs and (different) author names.

New publishers should submit on letterhead the following information to the Library of Congress, Attention: New CIP Participant, Cataloging in Publication Division, 101 Independence Avenue S.E., Washington, DC   20540-4320. You can also submit your material online at cip.loc.gov/cip/ecipp14.html   and cip.loc.gov/cip/ecip8.html. (PCN submissions can go to pcn.loc.gov/pcn.)

- Name, address, and homepage of the publisher

- Names, titles, email addresses, and phone numbers of the principal officers (Be sure you provide information on several officers.)

- ISBN numbers, book titles, and (several different) authors

- Evidence that the publisher is not self-publishing works authored by the publisher, and evidence that the publisher intends to publish the works of more than one or two authors, including photocopies of *just the front matter* of several forthcoming books.

- Evidence that the books will be marketed to a broad segment of the library market

- Catalogs or other promotional material

The initial application to the Library of Congress will take at least 30 days. Cataloging of subsequent books should take only two weeks, although the recent anthrax scare has the Library of Congress backed up for several months. Try to submit everything online to avoid delays. Don't forget to follow up with a printed copy of the book to the CIP office; they request this for final cataloging.

If you are having difficulties and need to speak to someone in person, you can email the following publisher liaisons at the CIP office:

Publisher	Liaison	Email
A-B	Schamell Padgett	spad@loc.gov
C-Do	Servon Gatewood	sgat@loc.gov

Dp-G	Cassandra Latney	clat@loc.gov
H-I	Nancy Andrews	nandrews@loc.gov
J-L	Dionne Simmons	dsim@loc.gov
M-N	Sherry McCoy	sgmcc@loc.gov
O-Pri	Tina Chubbs	tchu@loc.gov
Prj-Saint	Patricia Dyson	pdys@loc.gov
S	Lynn Souder	csou@loc.gov
T-U	Regina Thomas	mthomas@loc.gov
V-Z	Sonya Stewart	sste@loc.gov

Keep in mind that it may take several days (or weeks) to get a response to your email. For problems specifically relating to ECIP and EPCN, contact David Bucknum at dabu@loc.gov.

Quality Books, a non-exclusive distributor to libraries, also offers unofficial cataloging information for a fee, designed for publishing houses that haven't allowed enough time to get their cataloging data (or who can't get into the CIP program). Using Quality's cataloging, however, signals that your publishing house is small. Contact them at Quality Books, 1003 West Pines Road, Oregon, IL 61061, (815)732-4450 or (800)323-4241, fax (815)732-4499, Carolyn.Olson@Dawson.com.

Appendix E: Copyrights

The Library of Congress also issues copyrights. Your book is automatically copyrighted once you complete it—but you're still supposed to register it with the Library of Congress. The copyright protects everything in the text, including words and art, for your lifetime plus 50 years. The only thing not copyrighted is the title (which anyone can use.)

When the book is printed, send it to the copyright office with form TX (write and ask for this form) and $30. Write: Register of Copyrights, Library of Congress, Washington, DC 20559, (202)707-9100, `lcweb.loc.gov/copyright/`.

Appendix F: Wholesalers, Distributors and Fulfillment

The Publishing Game: Bestseller in 30 Days plan includes details on working with wholesalers. It does not include extensive details on distributors and fulfillment houses—because I don't believe you need them. To put your book into bookstores and libraries today requires using one or more of the wholesalers. However, contrary to conventional publishing wisdom, you can easily do your own distribution and fulfillment, and I encourage you to try this yourself—and reap the benefits.

Since there is much confusion amongst new publishers about these terms, let me clarify:

Ingram Book Company is the largest wholesaler in the country, and fills bookstore orders. Baker & Taylor is the second largest wholesaler, and fills some bookstore and many library orders. Neither do book publicity or promotion per se (though both offer mailings, advertisements, newsletter placements, and the like, all for fees) and until recently, neither did any distribution. Baker & Taylor just announced that it will be starting a distribution component as well, aimed mostly at $1 million plus independent publishers.

Both wholesalers request 55% discounts (that means they pay you 45% of list price), returnable terms, free freight in both directions (orders and returns), 90-day credit terms, and are not exclusive—all of which, though they hate to tell you this, is negotiable. Sign up with these wholesalers as quickly as possible when launching your book campaign—it is extremely difficult to do ongoing sales to libraries and bookstores without them.

- o **Ingram:** Publisher Relations Department, Ingram Distribution Group, One Ingram Boulevard, La Vergne, TN 37086, (615)287-5350 or (800)937-8222, extension 5250

- o **Baker & Taylor,** 44 Kirby Avenue, PO Box 734, Somerville, NJ 08876, (908)218-3803; fax (908)704-9460

- Another option is to make your books available to bookstores and libraries via a growing online wholesale option. At IndyBook you can buy a listing for $20/year plus a credit card processing fee of 5-12% depending on volume. Contact Bonnie Hayskar at info@IndyBook.com.

Distributors

Non-exclusive distributors are smaller versions of wholesalers, with very similar terms. They include BookPeople, New Leaf, Nutrifit/Royal and Quality Books. Some people claim that they sell more books by listing with these nonexclusive distributors—but I believe that as long as you're listed with both Ingram and Baker & Taylor, you will make most of these sales anyway. It's unclear whether forming arrangements with these companies is worth the time and energy you'll put in. One thing that is worthwhile, however, is to send your terms to those distributors that simply special order for libraries, so you don't lose potential library sales. Here's where to send your terms:

- The Book House, Inc., 208 W. Chicago Street, Jonesville, MI 49250, (517)849-2117, fax (517)849-4060, Bhinfo@TheBookHouse.com

- Brodart, 500 Arch Street, Williamsport, PA 17705, (800)233-8467

- Emery Pratt, 1966 W. Main Street, Owosso, MI 48867, (517)723-5291, fax (517)723-4677

- Midwest Library Service, 11443 St. Charles Rock Road, Bridgeton, MO 63044, (314)739-3100

- Quality Books, Carolyn Olson, 1003 West Pines Road, Oregon, IL 61061, (815)732-4450, fax (815)732-4499, Carolyn.Olson@Dawson.com

- Academic Book Center, 5600 NE Hassalo Street, Portland, OR 97213, (503)287-6657, fax (503)284-8859, info@acbc.com www.acbc.com

Exclusive Distributors take much of the headache—and much of the profit—out of independent publishing. If you can get an exclusive distributor—many independent publishers can't—they will take exclusive control of your books. They will be responsible for working with all the wholesalers, other distributors, bookstores, and libraries—not only will you not need to interact with anyone else in the book trade, you won't be able to legally. They will take your books directly from the printer, and distribute them to where they are going. In return for these services—which often include the use of a sales force to present your book to the chain stores, and inclusion of your book in their catalogues and at book shows—they take at least 65-68% of your sales. (Like wholesalers, they'll pay in 90 days, and like wholesalers, they want full returns.) Most exclusive distributors will also demand their hefty percentage of your online sales, including Amazon. Some publishers feel that the advantage of an exclusive distributor is their ease in getting your books into bookstores. (I feel that as long as they're allowed returns, you might regret this ease—and prefer to do your own, non-returnable, distribution.) It's also probably not worth considering an exclusive distributor if you have just a few titles and know your niche well. Exclusive distributors include:

- Publishers Group West, 1700 4th Street, Berkeley, CA 94710, (800)788-3123, fax (510)528-3444, info@pgw.com

- Independent Publishers Group, 814 North Franklin Street, Chicago, IL 60610, (312)337-0747, fax (312)337-5985, frontdesk@ipgbook.com

- Partners Book Distributing, 2325 Jarco Drive, Holt, MI 48842, (517)694-3205, fax (517)694-0617

- Biblio, 4720 Boston Way, Lanham, MD 20706, (301)459-3366, fax (301)459-1705

Independent Sales Representatives: If you think you'd like the help of a sales force, but are not interested in all the strings attached to using an exclusive distributor, consider hiring a sales representative on your own. You can find out more from the National Association of Independent Publishers

Representatives, 111 East 14th Street #157, New York, NY 10003, (508)877-5328, fax (508)788-0208, NAIPR@aol.com.

Fulfillment

Fulfillment Houses are not usually mentioned in the same breath as distributors and wholesalers, for no readily apparent reason. The job of a fulfillment house is to fulfill orders for your book. They do what the wholesalers do only on a micro-level—Barnes and Noble or a single bookstore will call a wholesaler and ask for books; individual readers will contact the fulfillment house and order a book. Fulfillment houses accept credit cards, answer their toll-free numbers, and generally charge a flat fee plus an additional percentage fee based on your volume. In addition to all the services of a wholesaler, they also store your books. Some fulfillment houses that we've heard about that are worth considering are:

- Rayve Productions, PO Box 726, Windsor, CA 95492, (707)838-6200, fax (707)838-2220, RayvePro@aol.com, www.Rayveproductions.com

- The Intrepid Group, 1331 Red Cedar Circle, Fort Collins, CO 80524, (970)493-3793, fax (970)493-8781, MediaDirector@IntrepidGroup.com

- Book Clearing House, 46 Purdy Street, Harrison, NY 10528, (800)431-1579, fax (914)853-0398, www.BookCH.com

- BookMasters, 2541 Ashland Road, Mansfield, OH 44905, (800)537-6727, fax (419)589-4040, www.BookMasters.com

Appendix G: Sample Budget

This is a sample budget, based on my expenses for producing and marketing my recent book, "Terrorism and Kids: Comforting Your Child," (www.TerrorismAndKids.com).

Keep in mind that I didn't have certain expenses (I already had basic office equipment and my publishing house was already set up); that I chose to do certain tasks rather than pay someone else to do them (answering my own telephone calls, order fulfillment); that I spend very little on advertising and not much more on publicity services (because I don't believe in spending much money on these items); and that my favorite expenditure is joining associations and attending conferences (but I'm currently marketing five books, so that cost, though listed below in its entirety, should really be amortized.)

Also keep in mind that I made certain decisions based on the nature of this book (that I needed to spend more to rush it into print quickly, incurring additional cover design expenses, for example) and on my understanding of the publishing industry (that I wouldn't sell these books returnable—which meant that fewer books were sold (since some libraries and bookstores won't buy books except on consignment)—but that I didn't have to worry about any of the "sold" books coming back six months later.

You don't need to spend exactly where I spent—and shouldn't, since every book, and every situation, is different--

but this will give you an idea of the sorts of budgetary decisions that need to be made, and the sorts of tradeoffs you can consider.

- Interior book design: Free--did it myself. If you don't have a good eye, this might be worth spending money on.

- Cover art: $2500. (Probably at least $1000 more than you will need to spend; this was a rush job as I went to press on September 11th to capitalize on the 9/11 market) from Mayapriya Long of BookWrights.com, one of the best cover artists in the business.

- Printing: As of March, 2002, I had printed 10,000 copies of the book, at a total cost of $12,000. This included the cost to matte laminate the cover of the books (I wouldn't do this with most books, but it looked right for this title) and to shrink-wrap in bundles of five (I find fewer books are damaged in storage and shipping if I shrink-wrap them).

- Shipping: Free. I happened to use a local printer and drove the books home in a minivan each print run. And all of my shipments to wholesalers are paid for by the wholesaler, because that is one of the terms I set. If you go with a standard contract you'll pay for that shipping (and the returns) and if you use a non-local printer, your shipping costs might run several hundred dollars per print run. Be sure to mention your organization memberships to get their shipping discounts.

- Galleys: $10. I sent only five galleys for this book, because I printed books one week after my manuscript was completed. Rather than go to the time and expense of having five galleys produced, I ripped covers off five finished books, and had them bound in cardboard at Kinko's. The cost of galleys can run as much as $15-20 per galley, and ordinarily you might need anywhere from ten to a hundred.

- Memberships: $500. I am a member of PMA, SPAN, Publishers Advocate, the American Booksellers Association, and several regional bookseller organizations. (I like organizations.)

- Contests: $200. I entered this book in PMA's Benjamin Franklin Awards for $60; Foreword Magazine's contest for $50; Independent Publishers contest for $60 and Parents' Choice award for $50. I highly recommend submitting your book for a Publishers Advocate award, since that is by far the cheapest contest entry around ($35), as well as a rolling process (so you can find out the results within a month after you submit your book, in time to get the award sticker incorporated into your book cover.)

- Book Displays: $260. I paid PMA to have the book displayed at Book Expo America, the Public Library Association show, and the Frankfurt Book

194 Appendix G: Sample Budget

Fair. I also displayed at several regional library association meetings, and several educational and psychological conferences.

- Postage: $700. I do spend a lot on postage, but this also included the postage costs for several other books, so it's hard to say how much of this I would have incurred just on this title.

- Postcards: $2500. This turned into one of my biggest ticket items for this book, since because of the timing, I paid other companies to do my mailings; often I label, stamp, and mail them myself. The postcards themselves usually cost only around $350 or $400 for 5,000 postcards total; the cost of the mailings (I did one mailing through one of the postcard places, and had Sam Decalo of Florida Academic Press do the others) was the remainder. The postcard was mailed to hundreds of independent publishers and libraries, generating book sales that are ongoing.

- Publicity: $1100. I spent about $150 buying media lists from Kate Bandos' a la carte publicity service; I spent $250 on Paul Krupin's fax service to over 1000 journalists; I spent $200 getting a subscription to PartyLine and another $500 on a subscription to Dan Jamal's PR Leads. As you can guess, I prefer a la carte publicity services, because I can control the money and get exactly the services I want. I also spent considerably more on this book than I usually do on publicity, because I was afraid the topical nature of the material would render the book obsolete before I could recoup my expenses if I didn't spend some more up front to move it faster. In retrospect, I wish I'd spent even more, especially earlier, and gotten the word out that much faster. But that decision varies from book to book.

- Conferences: $700. I attended PMA's Publishing University in New York, but since I was giving one of the talks, my conference tuition was waived, as was my entrance fee to Book Expo America. My total costs in NY (including accommodations and food) were about $700 (for the whole family). I made contact with dozens of movers and shakers in the publishing industry, so I consider it money well spent. (Unfortunately my three children, who spent a delightful few days acquiring free stuffed animals, novelty items, and wonderful books at Book Expo America, now want to go every year, which was not part of my budget!)

How did the book do? Well, I got reviews in American Library Association's BookList Magazine, Foreword Magazine, and several mentions in Publishers Weekly; I received quotes from notables including Senator Edward Kennedy; and the book received a 2002 American Booksellers Association BookSense selection and was nominated for a Parents Choice Award.

I sold 10,000 books in six months, and currently have a (large) quantity sale pending. My total gross income on each book was $6.72 on the ones I sold through wholesalers (many of them); on my non-wholesale sales my gross per book was much higher.   My total gross was well over $70,000. Accounting for my expenses, and not including taxes (and remember, these figures are slightly misleading because several of my expenses should have been amortized over all the books I am currently marketing), I netted approximately $50,000 in six months.

Just as a comparison: *The Infertility Diet: Get Pregnant and Prevent Miscarriage* on which I worked approximately five hours per week for the past three years, has sold over 10,000 books at $24.95 each (net $11.23 per book from wholesalers), grossing over $100,000 during that time.   It, too, continues to sell steadily.

You do the math.

Index

About the Author

Fern Reiss is an honors graduate from Harvard University with a degree in government. She writes frequently for major magazines, including Sesame Street, Scholastic Parent and Child, Moment, and Parade. She is the award-winning author of *Terrorism and Kids: Comforting Your Child*, *The Infertility Diet: Get Pregnant and Prevent Miscarriage*, *The Publishing Game: Publish a Book in 30 Days*, and *The Publishing Game: Find an Agent in 30 Days* all of which were published by Peanut Butter and Jelly Press, an independent publisher.

She is the founder of Publishers Advocate (www.PublishersAdvocate.com), an organization dedicated to maintaining a diversity of independent voices in publishing.

Fern consults with aspiring published authors, both those who want to find an agent and publisher, and those who want to publish independently. She speaks nationally on writing, publishing, and parenting, before groups as diverse as Publishers Marketing Association, the NY and Los Angeles Learning Annexes, and the New England Council of Child and Adolescent Psychiatry.

More information on Fern's books, speaking, and consulting can be found at the Peanut Butter and Jelly Press website, www.PBJPress.com.

Publishers Advocate

Publishers Advocate is an organization of independent publishers strongly committed to maintaining a diversity of independent voices in publishing, thereby ensuring America's Freedom of the Press. It aims to ensure this diversity by facilitating the financial survival of independent presses and by educating the book world about the importance of independent publishing.

To accomplish this mission, Publishers Advocate:

- Speaks out on issues that affect independent publishers, particularly financial issues, such as the industry practice of returns and the entry obstacles facing independent publishers, both of which we strongly oppose.

- Works with vendors and other associations to provide affordable tools and services to help members achieve financial success: Our vendor discounts currently include 5-20% off book printing prices for all members.

- Educates booksellers, librarians, and book lovers everywhere about the benefits of having a vibrant and healthy community of independent publishers, and the latest offerings of the independent press through weekly reviews of hot new books and related talks, an awards program, and an innovative Book of the Week Club.

Publishing Game Order Form

Yes, I want to create a bestseller... Send me:

___The Publishing Game: Bestseller in 30 Days $19.95
___The Publishing Game: Publish a Book in 30 Days $19.95
___The Publishing Game: Find an Agent in 30 Days $19.95

___**Literary Agents Kit**, $49—This Special Report details exactly how to get a literary agent. Includes hard-to-get contact information and email addresses for over 100 top literary agents.

___**Sell Your Books to Corporations Kit**, $49—Sell to Fortune 100 corporations. Letters, contracts, addresses (no emails).

___**Top Amazon Reviewers**, $49—Contact information (some addresses, some emails) for many top Amazon reviewers.

___**Independent Bookstore Publicity Kit**, $49—Contact independent bookstores directly! Includes emails and details.

___**Email Newsletter Kit** $49—Learn the fastest and best way to launch your own email newsletter. All the details you'll need.

___**Syndicate Yourself Kit** $49—Everything you need to know to syndicate your writing to newspapers nationwide!

___**Special Reports Kit** $49—All the details you need to know to learn how to sell special reports quickly and easily.

___**The whole enchilada!**—All seven special reports for $300.

Enclose $4 for priority mail ($10 outside the U.S.) & mail or fax your name, address, telephone, email, and credit card number including expiration date to:

Peanut Butter and Jelly Press, LLC
P.O. Box 590239, Newton, MA 02459-0002
(617)630-0945 phone/fax, orders@PublishingGame.com

For speediest service, please order directly from our website:
www.PublishingGame.com

Yes, I'd like to take advantage of the following opportunities through Publishers Advocate's email newsletter, distributed weekly to hundreds of booksellers, librarians, and adult education directors and booklovers nationwide:

____Announce galleys available for review or announce my book. $1/word (Emails and websites count as 2 words each.) Email ADS@PublishersAdvocate.com.

____Announce my talk. $1/word. You may want to include title of talk, speaker, ISBN, area of the country (please be specific and give the city closest to you), fee if any, length of your talk, what the program includes (e.g. talk, cooking demo, slide show, autographing), and contact info (email and phone). Email: ADS@PublishersAdvocate.com.

____Enter my book in the Publishers Advocate ongoing awards. $35. Add $10 rush fee and you'll hear back in 10 days.

____Book of the Week Buzz Club—To include your new title in our innovative program which introduces booklovers to independently published books at rock bottom prices, contact Buzz@PublishersAdvocate.com.

Join Publishers Advocate to participate in these special promotional opportunities and an ever-increasing array of benefits. You can become a member online at www.PublishersAdvocate.com. Or, sign up by sending your check for $50 to Publishers Advocate, PO Box 590239, Newton, MA 02459.